D0782617

The Broadview Pocket Guide to Writing
3/e

The Broadview Pocket Guide to Writing
3/e

Doug Babington, Don LePan, and Maureen Okun

broadview press

© 2009 Doug Babington, Don LePan, and Maureen Okun

All rights reserved. The use of any part of this publication reproduced, transmitted in any form or by any means, electronic, mechanical, photocopying, recording, or otherwise, or stored in a retrieval system, without prior written consent of the publisher—or in the case of photocopying, a licence from Acess Copyright (Canadian Copyright Licensing Agency), One Yonge Street, Suite 1900, Toronto, Ontario M5E 1E5—is an infringement of the copyright law.

Library and Archives Canada Cataloguing in Publication

Babington, Doug

The Broadview pocket guide to writing / Doug Babington, Don LePan, and Maureen Okun.—3rd ed.

Includes bibliographical references and index.

ISBN 978-1-55111-970-0

1. English language—Rhetoric—Textbooks. 2. English language—Grammar—Textbooks. 3. Report writing—Textbooks. 4. Bibliographical citations—Standards—Textbooks. I. LePan, Don, 1954- II. Okun, Maureen Jeannette, 1961- III. Title.

LB2369.B24 2009   808'.042   C2009-902303-2

Broadview Press is an independent, international publishing house, incorporated in 1985. Broadview believes in shared ownership, both with its employees and with the general public; since the year 2000 Broadview shares have traded publicly on the Toronto Venture Exchange under the symbol BDP.

We welcome comments and suggestions regarding any aspect of our publications—please feel free to contact us at the addresses below or at broadview@broadviewpress.com.

North America:

PO Box 1243, Peterborough, Ontario, Canada K9J 7H5

2215 Kenmore Ave., Buffalo, NY, USA, 14207

Tel: (705) 743-8990; Fax: (705) 743-8353

email: customerservice@broadviewpress.com

UK, Ireland, and continental Europe:

NBN International, Estover Road, Plymouth, UK, PL6 7PY

Tel: 44 (0) 1752 202300; Fax: 44 (0) 1752 202330

email: enquiries@nbninternational.com

Australia and New Zealand:

NewSouth Books

c/o TL Distribution

15–23 Helles Ave., Moorebank, NSW, 2170

Tel: (02) 8778 9999; Fax: (02) 8778 9944

email: orders@tldistribution.com.au

www.broadviewpress.com

BROADVIEW PRESS ACKNOWLEDGES THE FINANCIAL SUPPORT OF THE GOVERNMENT OF CANADA THROUGH THE BOOK PUBLISHING INDUSTRY DEVELOPMENT PROGRAM (BPIDP) FOR OUR PUBLISHING ACTIVITIES.

This book is printed on paper containing 100% post-consumer fibre.

PRINTED IN CANADA

HOW TO USE THIS BOOK

The goal of *The Broadview Pocket Guide to Writing* is to provide a concise reference text that is easy to use in every respect. We've made the book easy to carry around, and easy to use lying flat on a desk. We've also tried to keep the organization simple so that the book will be easy for you to find your way round in. There are two ways to locate information in the text:

- **index**: Go to the index at the back of the book to find the location in the book for any topic, large or small.

- **table of contents**: The detailed table of contents at the beginning of the book sets out the sections, chapters, and headings within chapters.

In order to keep the book concise and convenient, we have not included any sample essays, but you may find several of these on the Broadview Press adjunct writing website:

- **sample essays**, providing examples of essay style and structure, as well as examples of different referencing styles (APA, Chicago, and CSE as well as MLA), are available through the Broadview Press website; go to www.broadviewpress.com, and click on LINKS.

For the third edition we have updated our coverage of the various systems of citation and reference; we include the same comprehensive coverage of MLA, APA, Chicago, and CSE styles as is provided in the full *Broadview Guide to Writing*.

This book does not provide one feature that you will find in many other writing reference books: highlights in blue or red or green throughout the book. Largely because the text is printed in one colour, however, the publisher is able to offer *The Broadview Pocket Guide to Writing* at a substantially lower price than most other texts; this is one other respect in which we hope *The Broadview Pocket Guide to Writing* will be a truly student-friendly text.

Contents

GRAMMAR 33

PUNCTUATION

CLEAR WRITING

A Checklist

1. CHOOSING THE BEST WORDS

1a. BE AS CLEAR AND SPECIFIC AS POSSIBLE

Clear writing resists vagueness and employs academic jargon only when it helps to clarify meaning.

needs checking	Several key components of this issue will be identified in this essay, and various facets of each will be discussed.
revised	This essay will look at three things.
needs checking	They wanted the plan to be optimally functional.
revised	They wanted the plan to work well.
needs checking	In an economic slow down the economy declines.
revised	In an economic slow down the rate of growth in the economy declines.

1b. WATCH FOR REDUNDANCY

Redundancies are words or expressions that repeat in another way a meaning already expressed. Sometimes they may be useful to add emphasis; usually they should be avoided.

needs checking	The house is very large in size.
revised	The house is very large.
needs checking	It would be mutually beneficial for both countries.
revised	It would be beneficial for both countries.

1c. AVOID WORDINESS

In groping for ideas at the rough draft stage, writers often latch on to unnecessarily complex or wordy sentence structures.

needs checking   As regards the trend in interest rates, it is likely to continue to be upward.

revised   Interest rates are likely to continue to rise.

needs checking   There are many historians who accept this thesis.

revised   Many historians accept this thesis.

1d. WATCH FOR MISSING PARTS

It is easy to omit a word or a link in an argument.

needs checking   She told Felicity and about the accident.

revised   She told Felicity and me about the accident.

needs checking   She reminded the conference that just one intercontinental ballistic missile could plant 200 million trees.

revised   She reminded the conference that the money spent on just one intercontinental ballistic missile could be used to plant 200 million trees.

1e. CHOOSE THE BEST VERB

If you want to keep the focus on the *recipient* of an action rather than on its *agent*, the passive voice is useful. In other situations, the active voice is less wordy and more effective.

needs checking   The election was lost by the Premier.
(Passive voice—7 words)

revised   The Premier lost the election.
(Active voice—5 words)

needs checking	I added 50 millilitres of the solution to the serum.
revised	Fifty millilitres of the solution were added to the serum.

(In reporting on a scientific experiment the focus should be kept on the actions, not on the particular individuals performing them.)

2. ORDER AND CONNECT YOUR IDEAS

The order in which you make your ideas appear and the ways in which you connect them—and show your reader how they connect—are as important to good writing as the ideas themselves.

2a. PARAGRAPHING

There is a degree of flexibility when it comes to the matter of where and how often to start new paragraphs. Sometimes a subtle point in an argument will require a paragraph of almost an entire page to elaborate; occasionally a single sentence can form an effective paragraph. Yet separating ideas into paragraphs remains an important aid to the processes of both reading and writing. Following are some guidelines as to when it is appropriate to begin a new paragraph.

a) in narration:

• whenever the story changes direction ("This was the moment Preston Manning had been waiting for...," "When Napoleon left Elba he...")

• when there is a gap in time in the story ("Two weeks later the issue was raised again in cabinet...")

b) in description:

• whenever you switch from describing one place, person, or thing to describing another ("Even such a brief description as this is enough to give some sense of the city and its pretensions. Much more interesting in many ways are some of British Columbia's smaller cities and towns...")

c) in persuasion or argument:

- when a new topic is introduced ("There can be little doubt that Austen's asides on the literary conventions of her time provide an amusing counterpoint to her story. But does this running commentary detract from the primary imaginative experience of *Northanger Abbey*?")

- when there is a change in direction of the argument ("To this point we have been looking only at the advantages of a guaranteed annual income. We should also ask, however, whether or not it would be practical to implement.")

d) when changing from one mode to another:

- Description, narration, and argument are commonly blended together in writing. If, for example, a text moves from describing an experiment to analysing its significance, it's a good time to start a new paragraph. If it moves from telling where Napoleon went and what he did to discussing why events unravelled in this way, the same holds true.

2b. JOINING WORDS

The art of combining correct clauses and sentences logically and coherently is as much dependent on taking the time to think through what we are writing as it is on knowledge of correct usage. It is important to use appropriate joining words to help the reader see how ideas are linked—and important as well not to give too many or contradictory cues to the reader. Almost no writer manages these things (let alone perfect grammar and spelling!) the first time. Good writers typically write at least two or three drafts of any piece of writing before considering it finished.

needs checking At the end of World War II there was substantial optimism that the application of Keynesian analysis would lead to economic stability and security. Over the post-war period optimistic rationalism weakened in the face of reality.

This passage gives the reader too few cues. It is not immediately clear how the idea of the first sentence is connected to that of the second. The problem is readily solved by the addition of a single word:

revised

At the end of World War II there was substantial optimism that the application of Keynesian analysis would lead to economic stability and security. Over the post-war period, however, optimistic rationalism weakened in the face of reality.

needs checking

A short report in which you request an increase in your department's budget should be written in the persuasive mode. Most reports, however, do not have persuasion as their main objective. Persuasion, though, will often be one of their secondary objectives. In reports like these, some parts will be written in the persuasive mode.

Here, the use of *however* and *though* in consecutive sentences gives the reader the sense of twisting back and forth without any clear sense of direction. This sort of difficulty can be removed by rewording or rearranging the ideas:

revised

A short report in which you request an increase in your department's budget should be written in the persuasive mode. Most reports, however, do not have persuasion as their main objective. Persuasion will thus be at most a secondary objective.

The use of joining words is complicated by grammar; certain joining words are used to show how the ideas of one sentence connect to those of the previous sentence, while others are used to connect ideas in the same sentence. Words commonly used to connect the ideas of different sentences:

as a result,	further,
however,	furthermore,
in addition,	nevertheless,

Words commonly used to connect ideas within the same sentence:

although	though
and	whereas
because	while

(NB These lists are far from exhaustive.)

needs checking   There will not be regular delivery service this Friday, however, regular service will resume Monday.

revised   There will not be regular delivery service this Friday. However, regular service will resume Monday.

or   There will not be regular delivery service this Friday, but regular service will resume Monday.

ON THE WEB

Exercises on joining words may be found at **www.broadviewpress.com/writing**.

Click on **Exercises** and go to **C14–C46**.

Because: The joining word *because* is a particularly troublesome one. It is easy to become turned around and use *because* to introduce a result or an example rather than a cause.

needs checking	He had been struck by a car because he lay bleeding in the road.
revised	We could infer that he had been struck by a car because we saw him lying bleeding in the road.

(This follows the causal connections of the writer's thought processes, but is wordy and cumbersome.)

revised	He lay bleeding on the road; evidently he had been struck by a car.
or	He had been struck by a car and lay bleeding on the road.

needs checking	The Suharto regime detained people in jail without trial because it had little respect for the law.
revised	We may conclude that the Suharto regime had little respect for the law because we know it detained people in jail without trial.

(Again, this follows the causal connections of the writer's thought processes, but is wordy and cumbersome.)

revised	The fact that the Suharto regime detained people for long periods without ever bringing them to trial shows that it had little respect for the law.
or	The Suharto regime in Indonesia showed little respect for the law. It detained people for long periods, for example, without ever bringing them to trial.
or	The Suharto regime in Indonesia had little respect for the law; it detained people for long periods without ever bringing them to trial.

2c. ORDER AND WEIGHT YOUR IDEAS ACCORDING TO THEIR IMPORTANCE

The order in which ideas appear in any piece of writing, and the space that is devoted to them, will inevitably send signals to the reader as to their relative importance. For this reason, it is wise to avoid long discussions of matters you consider to be of less importance—or else to relegate them to a note outside the main body of the text. Similarly, it is wise to signal through the amount of space you give to your main ideas your sense of their importance. (Obviously you may also signal this through the use of words and phrases such as *most importantly...*, *crucially....*) You should be sure as well to give the reader a clear sense in the opening and closing paragraphs of the direction of the piece of writing.

2d. WATCH FOR AMBIGUITY

Inappropriate word order may often cause confusion as to how ideas are connected.

needs checking   The macadamia was named for Dr. John MacAdam, an enthusiastic scientist who promoted the nut in its native Australia, and was dubbed "the perfect nut" by Luther Burbank.

revised   The macadamia was named for Dr. John MacAdam, an enthusiastic scientist who promoted the nut in its native Australia. Luther Burbank referred to the macadamia as "the perfect nut."

> ## RED TAPE HOLDS UP NEW BRIDGE
>
> The following are all examples of ambiguity in newspaper headlines. In some cases it may take several moments to decipher the intended meaning.
>
> ### TWO PEDESTRIANS STRUCK BY BRIDGE
>
> ### MAN HELD OVER GIANT L.A. BRUSH FIRE
>
> ### ILLEGAL ALIENS CUT IN HALF BY NEW LAW
>
> ### PASSERBY INJURED BY POST OFFICE
>
> ### RED TAPE HOLDS UP NEW BRIDGE
>
> ### VILLAGE WATER HOLDS UP WELL
>
> ### JERK INJURES NECK, WINS AWARD
>
> ### BISHOP THANKS GOD FOR CALLING
>
> (The above examples come courtesy of columnist Bob Swift of Knight-Ridder Newspapers, and of Prof. A. Levey of the University of Calgary.)
>
> And, from the Global News weather telecast, the following gem:
>
> ### "OUT WEST TOMORROW, THEY'RE GOING TO SEE THE SUN, AS WELL AS ATLANTIC CANADA."
>
> (Who ever suggested that Canadians lacked vision?)

3. MAKING YOUR WRITING CONSISTENT

3a. AGREEMENT AMONG THE GRAMMATICAL PARTS OF YOUR WRITING

In order to be consistent, the various parts of your writing must be in agreement grammatically. Fuller treatment of this subject appears below in the section on grammar; here are a few examples of the sorts of problems that can arise:

needs checking   The state of Afghanistan's roads reflect the chaotic situation.

revised   The state of Afghanistan's roads reflects the chaotic situation.

(Here the writer has made the mental error of thinking of *roads* as the subject of the verb *reflect*, whereas in fact the subject is the singular noun *state*.)

needs checking A diplomat represents his or her country in its dealings with other countries. They often help to negotiate treaties and other agreements.

revised Diplomats represent their country in its dealings with other countries. They often help to negotiate treaties and other agreements.

(The pronoun *they* at the beginning of the second sentence needs to agree grammatically with the noun to which it refers.)

needs checking We went over to the woman lying on the pavement; she looked either dead or asleep. Suddenly she sits bolt upright.

revised We went over to the woman lying on the pavement; she looked either dead or asleep. Suddenly she sat bolt upright.

(The revised passage is written consistently in the past tense.)

needs checking Unlike the first version of the novel, which appeared in a weekly newspaper, Stowe had a chance to review the galley proofs of the 1852 edition.

revised Whereas Stowe did not have a chance to proof the first version of the novel, which appeared in a weekly newspaper, she was able to review the galley proofs of the 1852 edition.

(The grammatical structure of the first of these sentences suggests that a novel can read itself.)

ON THE WEB

Exercises on subject-verb agreement may be found at
www.broadviewpress.com/writing.
Click on **Exercises** and go to **A2**.

3b. WATCH FOR MIXED METAPHORS

Using metaphors can help to convey your ideas more clearly to the reader—and help to make your writing more interesting. A mixed metaphor occurs when we are not really thinking of the meaning of the words we use. "If we bite the bullet we have to be careful not to throw the baby out with the bathwater." "We will leave no stone unturned as we search for an avenue through which the issue may be resolved." As soon as one really thinks about such sentences one realises that the bullet is really better off out of the baby's bathwater, and that the best way to search for an avenue is not to turn stones over.

needs checking   Now the President is out on a limb, and some of his colleagues are pulling the rug out from under him.

revised   Now the President is out on a limb, and some of his colleagues are preparing to saw it off.

4. RHYTHM AND VARIETY

The most predictable syntax in the grammar of English is SUBJECT-PREDICATE, as in the sentence "The effects are disturbing." Upend that predictability, and you are on your way to rhythmical distinctiveness: "Less obvious, but equally disturbing, are the effects this work could have in...."

An important element in rhythmical distinctiveness is balance. Sometimes a pleasing effect may be achieved simply by repeating grammatical structures: "We may not wish to deny Rushton the rights to publish such research. Nor can we deny the harm that it causes." Sometimes balance may be achieved by placing words or phrases in apposition: "Haldemann was Nixon's closest confidante, his most influential advisor."

Often paired connectives ("if...then," "either...or," "not only...but also") can help in achieving balance. As always, the writer must be careful to put the words in the right places.

needs checking	Hardy was not only a prolific novelist but wrote poetry too, and also several plays.
revised	Hardy was not only a prolific novelist but also a distinguished poet and a dramatist.

needs checking	The experiment can either be performed with hydrogen or with oxygen.
revised	The experiment can be performed with either hydrogen or oxygen.
	(The choice is between the two gases, not between performing and some other thing.)

needs checking	To subdue Iraq through sanctions, he felt, was better than using force.
revised	To subdue Iraq through sanctions, he felt, was better than to use force.
	(The infinitive *to subdue* is balanced by the infinitive *to use*.)

Even careful balancing cannot make a steady diet of long sentences palatable; a rich source of rhythm in any well written essay is the short sentence. When revising their work, careful writers look to balance long sentences and short ones—and to notice such things as a preponderance of "there is..." and "it is..." sentences.

needs checking	It is important to consider the cultural as well as the economic effects of globalization. In the past few years there have been many people who have argued that these would be even more significant, and would inevitably cause the disappearance of many nations as distinct cultural entities.

revised   Globalization has cultural as well as
                 economic effects. In the past few years
                 many have argued that these are even
                 more significant, and that they will
                 eventually cause the disappearance of
                 many nations as distinct cultural entities.

5. TONE, VOICE, AND SPECIAL WRITING SITUATIONS

5a. ACADEMIC WRITING

Academic writing often depends upon the use of
jargon—namely, the specialized language of any
scholarly field. Inevitably, such language will sometimes
present challenges, and communication is always made
easier to the extent that the writer is able to express
ideas in the most straightforward manner possible. The
goal is to balance the requirements of the academic
discipline with those of communication—to write in a
varied and flexible style, one that utilizes simple words
wherever possible without becoming simplistic.

The tone of academic writing is typically one of
careful argument. The aim is to persuade the reader
through logic and through the marshalling of evidence
(rather than, for example, through attempting to exhort or
entertain the reader). It is thus always important when
writing in an academic context to provide support for
whatever claims you make, and to be careful in how you
phrase those claims. Almost all academic writers rely
heavily on words and on phrases such as *for the most
part, mainly, tends to...,* and so on, in order to ensure
that the claims they are making allow for some
exceptions. Conversely, they generally avoid words such
as *always* and *never*, which would leave their arguments
open to being refuted through a single exception.

Most academic essays are formal pieces of writing,
and should be approached as such. Readers expect a
calm and disinterested tone, free of extreme emotion and

of slang or conversational usage. That should not be taken to imply that thinking rigorously about a topic precludes feeling strongly about it—or conveying to the reader how the writer feels. But usually it is advisable to try to do this without employing first-person singular pronouns; most academic writers use *I* or *me* infrequently, if at all. Most academic writers aim to succeed in persuading their readers by letting the evidence speak for itself. Thus, many instructors advise their students to entirely avoid the use of first-person pronouns.

As with all guidelines to style and tone, though, this one should not be regarded as written in stone. George Orwell, often praised as the finest essayist of the twentieth century, uses *I* and *me* frequently.

5b. WRITING ABOUT LITERATURE

One sort of convention in academic writing that can take some getting used to is the way in which verb tenses are used. Many students find writing about literature particularly challenging in this respect; its conventions present fundamental problems for the student at the level of sentence structure.

The past tense is, of course, normally used to name actions which happened in the past. But when one is writing about what happens in a work of literature, convention decrees that we use the simple present tense.

needs checking	Romeo fell in love with Juliet as soon as he saw her.
revised	Romeo falls in love with Juliet as soon as he sees her.
needs checking	In her short stories, Alice Munro explored both the outer and the inner worlds of small town life.
revised	In her short stories, Alice Munro explores both the outer and the inner worlds of small town life.

If literature in its historical context is being discussed, however, the simple past tense is usually the best choice:

needs checking	Shakespeare writes *Romeo and Juliet* when he was about thirty years of age.
revised	Shakespeare wrote *Romeo and Juliet* when he was about thirty years of age.
needs checking	Alice Munro wins the Governor General's Award for the first time in 1968, for her collection *Dance of the Happy Shades*.
revised	Alice Munro won the Governor General's Award for the first time in 1968, for her collection *Dance of the Happy Shades*.

In some circumstances either the past or the present tense may be possible in a sentence, depending on the context:

correct	In her early work Munro often explored themes relating to adolescence. (appropriate if the focus is on historical developments relating to the author)
also correct	In her early work Munro often explores themes relating to adolescence. (appropriate if the focus is on the work itself)

Notice that if the subject of a sentence is the work itself, the present tense is required:

needs checking	Munro's early work often explored themes relating to adolescence.
revised	Munro's early work often explores themes relating to adolescence.

Often in an essay about literature the context may require shifting back and forth between past and present tenses. In the following passage, for example, the present tense is used except for the sentence that recounts the historical fact of Eliot refusing permission:

> T.S. Eliot's most notorious expression of anti-Semitism is the opinion he expresses in *After Strange Gods* that in "the society that we desire," "any large number of free-thinking Jews" would be "undesirable" (64). Tellingly, Eliot never allowed *After Strange Gods* to be reprinted. But his anti-Semitism emerges repeatedly in his poetry as well. In "Gerontion," for example, he describes...

In such cases even experienced writers have to think carefully during the revision process about the most appropriate tense for each verb. Note in the following example the change in verb tense from *was* to *is*.

needs checking

In *The Two Gentleman of Verona* Shakespeare exhibited a degree of technical accomplishment unprecedented in the English drama. He still had much to learn as a dramatist and as a poet; in its wit or its power to move us emotionally *The Two Gentlemen of Verona* was at an enormous remove from the great works of a few years later. But already, in 1592, Shakespeare had mastered all the basic techniques of plot construction that were to sustain the structures of the great plays.

revised

In *The Two Gentleman of Verona* Shakespeare exhibits a degree of technical accomplishment unprecedented in the English drama. He still had much to learn as a dramatist and as a poet; in its wit or its power to move us emotionally *The Two Gentlemen of Verona* is at an enormous remove from the great works of a few years later. But already, in 1592, Shakespeare had mastered all the basic techniques of plot construction that were to sustain the structures of the great plays.

consistency in verb tense when integrating quotations: If one is writing about literature the writing will usually be in the *present* tense, but the quotations one wishes to use are likely to be in the *past* tense. Often it is thus necessary, if you are incorporating a quotation into a sentence, to rephrase and/or adjust the length of the quotation in order to preserve grammatical consistency. If a quotation is set apart from the body of your own writing, on the other hand, you do not need to (and should not) rephrase.

needs checking Emma Bovary lives largely through memory and fantasy. She daydreams frequently, and, as she reads, "the memory of the Vicomte kept her happy" (244).

(The past tense *kept* is inconsistent with the present tense *reads* and *daydreams*.)

revised Emma Bovary lives largely through memory and fantasy. She daydreams frequently, and, as she reads, the "memory of the Vicomte" (244) keeps her happy.

or Emma Bovary lives largely through memory and fantasy. She daydreams frequently, and blends fact and fiction in her imaginings: "Always, as she read, the memory of the Vicomte kept her happy. She established a connection between him and the characters of her favorite fiction" (244).

5c. WRITING IN OTHER ACADEMIC DISCIPLINES

To a large extent the same principles that are used in writing about literature apply in other disciplines. In many other disciplines the present tense is the tense most commonly used. Indeed, if you are treating the ideas you are discussing as "live" ideas, it is wrong to use the past tense:

needs checking	In an important recent book, Nelly Ferguson surveyed the history of the decline of empires, and predicted that during the course of the twenty-first century China will replace the United States as the world's leading power.
revised	In an important recent book, Nelly Ferguson surveys the history of the decline of empires, and predicts that during the course of the twenty-first century China will replace the United States as the world's leading power.
needs checking	In their 2009 paper Smith and Johnson suggested that parental influence is more important than that of peers, even for adolescents. This essay will examine these claims and assess their validity.
revised	In their 2009 paper Smith and Johnson suggest that parental influence is more important than that of peers, even for adolescents. This essay will examine these claims and assess their validity.

In many disciplines, particularly in the sciences, it is also common to use the present perfect tense when discussing relevant recent research:

Although research has often found the attitude-to-behavior connection to be quite weak, the behavior-to-attitude link has been shown to be quite strong. As Festinger (2005) and Kiesler, Nisbet and Zanna (2009) have demonstrated, an asymmetry exists between the two possible directions. As Acheson (2008) has put it, "we are...very good at finding reasons for what we do, but not very good at doing what we find reasons for" (25).

It is important to remember that the use of the present tense in academic writing is not dependent on how recently the ideas being discussed were first put forward; the key thing is whether or not you are discussing them as live ideas today. You may use the present tense when discussing a paper written six months ago—but you may also use the present tense when discussing a text dating from twenty-four centuries ago. Just as you may say when writing about literature that Shakespeare *explores* the potentially corrosive effects of ambition, so too you may say that Aristotle *approaches* ethical questions with a view as much to the virtue of the doer as to the rightness of the deed, and that Marx *values* highly the economic contribution of labour—even though Shakespeare and Aristotle and Marx are themselves long dead. As with the text of a story or poem, the writings of dead thinkers may be discussed as embodying live thoughts—ideas that may retain interest and relevance.

Conversely, if the ideas you are discussing are being considered historically rather than as of current relevance, you should not use the present tense.

needs checking   The renowned astronomer Fred Hoyle advances arguments against the big bang theory of the origin of the universe. Hoyle suggests that the universe perpetually regenerates itself. (Hoyle's arguments have now been refuted.)

revised   The renowned astronomer Fred Hoyle advanced arguments against the big bang theory of the origin of the

universe. Hoyle suggested that the
universe perpetually regenerates itself.

As is the case with writing about literature, academic
writing in disciplines such as history or philosophy or
political science may often look at a text *both* from a
historical perspective *and* from the perspective of the live
ideas that are put forward within it. In such
circumstances the writer needs to be prepared to shift
verb tenses depending on the context:

purely historical context

Darwin finally published his theory
only after an article by Alfred Wallace
advancing a similar theory had been
published. The central element in
Darwin's theory was the concept of
natural selection. Unlike Wallace,
Darwin had become convinced that...

historical context + *live ideas*

Darwin finally published his theory
only after an article by Alfred Wallace
advancing a similar theory had been
published. The central element in
Darwin's theory is the concept of
natural selection; according to Darwin's
theory, all organisms are...

purely historical context

Hobbes believed that the tragic
upheaval of the English civil war was
caused by the spread of dangerous
beliefs about humans and human
society. Hobbes's view was that humans
require a structure of government to
enforce a structure of laws; otherwise, he
felt, they would revert to a state of
nature in which life would be "nasty,
brutish, and short." Hobbes's

opponents did not disagree with the substance of this notion. But because he had argued from first principles rooted in human realities rather than in any divine ordering, he was accused of atheism, and threatened with prosecution...

historical context + live ideas

Hobbes firmly believed that the tragic upheaval of the English civil war was caused by the spread of dangerous beliefs about humans and human society. Hobbes's view is that humans require a structure of government to enforce a structure of laws; otherwise they revert to a state of nature in which life will be "nasty, brutish, and short." That central notion still lies at the core of much political theory today...

ON THE WEB

Exercises on choosing the correct tense may be found at

www.broadviewpress.com/writing.

Click on **Exercises** and go to **D51–D52**.

5d. BUSINESS WRITING

Tone may be the most important aspect of business writing. The adjective *businesslike* conjures up images of efficiency and professional distance, and certainly it is appropriate to convey those qualities in most business reports, memos, and correspondence. In a great deal of business writing, however, it is also desirable to convey a warm, personal tone; striking the right balance between the personal and the professional is at the heart of the art of business writing. Following are a few guidelines.

Consult your colleagues. Circulate a draft of any important document to others and ask their opinion. Is

the tone too cold and formal? Is it too gushy and enthusiastic? Is it too direct? Or not direct enough?

Be careful about suggesting you are speaking for your entire organization. Unless you are sure, you are well advised to qualify any extreme statements.

needs checking	Our organization underprices every competitor.
revised	In my experience our prices are lower than those of major competitors.

needs checking	There is no way we would ever cut back on research and development.
revised	As an organization we have a strong commitment to research and development.

Given that most business communication operates within a hierarchical power structure, it is particularly important to foreground consideration in business memos, letters, and emails. Avoid direct commands wherever possible; give credit to others when things go right; and take responsibility and apologize when things go wrong.

needs checking	Here is the material we spoke of. Send the report in by the end of the month to my attention.
revised	I enclose the material we spoke of. If you could send in the report by the end of the month to my attention, I'd be very grateful.

needs checking	I am writing in response to your complaint. We carry a large number of products with similar titles, and sometimes errors in shipping occur. Please in future specify the ISBN of the item you are ordering, as that will help keep errors to a minimum.
revised	Thank you for your letter—and my sincere apologies on behalf of our

company for our mistake. As you may know, we carry a large number of products with similar titles, and (particularly in cases where our customer service department is not able to double check against an ISBN) errors do sometimes occur. But that is an explanation rather than an excuse; I *do* apologize, and I have asked that the correct item be shipped to you immediately. Thank you for drawing this matter to my attention.

5e. SLANG AND INFORMAL ENGLISH

Many words and expressions often used in conversation are considered inappropriate in formal English. Here is a short list of words and expressions to avoid in formal writing:

AVOID	REPLACE WITH
anyways	anyway
awfully	very, extremely
boss	manager, supervisor
bunch	group
(except for grapes, bananas etc.)	
buy	bargain
(as a noun—"a good buy")	
kid	child, girl, boy
kind of, sort of	rather, in some respects
lots of	a great deal of
mad	angry
(unless to mean "insane")	
have got	have, own
go (to mean "say")	say

All contractions (it's, he's, there's, we're, etc.) should be avoided in formal writing, as should conversational markers such as *like* and *well*.

needs checking   Let's say for example unemployment

got much worse, the government
would need to act.

revised   If, for example, unemployment became
much worse, the government would
need to act.

6. BIAS-FREE USAGE

6a. GENDER

The healthy revolution in attitudes towards gender roles
in recent generations has created some awkwardness in
English usage—though not nearly so much as some have
claimed. *Chair* is a simple non-sexist replacement for
chairman, as is *business people* for *businessmen*. Nor is
one forced into *garbageperson* or *policeperson*; *police
officer* and *garbage collector* are entirely
unobjectionable even to the linguistic purist. *Fisher* is a
good replacement for *fisherman*; here again, there is no
need for the -person suffix.

The use of *mankind* to mean *humanity*, and of *man*
to mean *human being*, have for some years been rightly
frowned upon. (Ironically enough, *man* originally had
human being as its **only** meaning; in Old English a
werman was a male adult human being, a *wifman* a
female.) A remarkable number of adults still cling to
sexist usages, however, and even still try to convince
themselves that it is possible to use *man* in a gender-
neutral fashion.

Well, why **can't** *man* be gender neutral? To start
with, because of the historical baggage such usage
carries with it. Here, for example, is what the best-selling
novelist Grant Allen had to say on the topic in a
magazine called *Forum* in 1889:

In man, I would confidently assert, as biological fact,
the males are the race; the females are merely the sex
told off to recruit and reproduce it. All that is
distinctly human is man—the field, the ship, the

mine, the workshop; all that is truly woman is merely reproductive—the home, the nursery, the schoolroom.

But the baggage is not merely historical; much of the problem remains embedded in the language today. A useful litmus test is how sex and gender differences are approached. Look, for example, at this sentence from the Sept. 14, 1996 issue of *The Economist*:

One of the most basic distinctions in human experience—that between men and women—is getting blurrier and blurrier.

Now let's try the same sentence using *man's* instead of *human*:

One of the most basic distinctions in man's experience—that between men and women—is getting blurrier and blurrier.

In this sort of context we are all forced to sense that something is amiss. We have to realise when we see such examples that *man* and *he* and even *mankind* inevitably carry with them some whiff of maleness; they can never fully and fairly represent all of humanity. (If they didn't carry with them some scent of maleness it wouldn't be possible to make a joke about the difficulty of turning *men* into *human beings*.) Most contexts are of course more subtle than this, and it is thus often easy for humans—but especially for men—not to notice that the male terms always carry with them connotations that are not gender-neutral. *Humanity, humans, people*—these words are not in any way awkward or jargon-ridden; let's use them.

To replace *man* with *humanity* is not inherently awkward to even a slight degree. But the pronouns are more difficult. Clearly the consistent use of *he* to represent both sexes is unacceptable. Yet *he/she, s/he,* or *he or she* are undeniably awkward. *S/he* is quite functional on the printed page, but defies translation into oral English.

Another solution is to avoid the singular pronoun as much as possible either by repeating nouns ("An architect should be aware of the architect's clients' budgets as well as the architect's grand schemes") or by switching to the plural ("Architects should be aware of their clients' budgets as well as their own grand schemes"). Of these two the second is obviously preferable. In longer works some prefer a third strategy that eliminates awkwardness entirely: to alternate between the masculine pronoun *he* and the feminine pronoun *she* when referring to a single, generic member of a group. Using *she* to refer to, say, an architect, or a professor, or a sports star, or a prime minister can have the salutary effect of reminding readers or listeners that there is nothing inherently male in these occupations. In a short piece of writing, however, it can be distracting to the reader if there are several bounces back and forth between female and male in the same paragraph. And a cautionary note should accompany this strategy even when it may conveniently be employed; be **very** careful not to assign *he* to all the professors, executives, or doctors, and *she* to all the students, secretaries, or nurses.

Pronouns: Undoubtedly the most troublesome questions for those who are concerned both about gender equality and about good English arise over situations involving singular pronouns such as *everyone, anyone, anybody, somebody, someone, no one, each, either, neither*. It can be difficult enough to re-cast sentences involving such words so that everything agrees, even before the issue of gender enters the picture.

> Everybody felt that the film was better than any other they had seen that year.

According to the rules most of us have been taught, that sentence is wrong; *everybody* is singular, and *they* must therefore be changed:

> Everybody felt that the film was better than any other she had seen that year.

Everybody felt that the film was better than any other he had seen that year.

Everybody felt that the film was better than any other she or he had seen that year.

But, as Robertson Cochrane has pointed out ("Sex and the Single Pronoun," *The Globe and Mail*, May 1992), the insistence on the singularity of such pronouns is a relatively recent phenomenon, dating from the codification of English grammar that took root in the eighteenth century. Before that time Chaucer, Shakespeare, Swift, and the rest had no qualms about using *they* or *their* to refer to *anyone* and *everyone*. Cochrane persuasively argues that returning to the ways of Chaucer and Shakespeare in this respect is better than constantly trying "to write around the pronoun problem, and [it is] certainly less offensive than arrogantly and 'properly' applying masculine labels to all of humankind."

inappropriate	Mankind cannot bear too much reality.
gender neutral	Human kind cannot bear too much reality.
inappropriate	Everyone will have a chance to express
(though 'correct')	his views before the meeting is over.
gender neutral	Everyone will have a chance to express their views...

Of course issues of gender are not confined to the right word choice. Consider the following descriptions of political candidates with essentially the same backgrounds:

Carla Jenkins, a lawyer and a School Board Trustee, is also the mother of three lovely daughters.

George Kaplan, a lawyer and a School Board Trustee, has a long record of public service in the region.

• • •

George Kaplan, a lawyer and a School Board Trustee, is also the father of three lovely daughters.

Carla Jenkins, a lawyer and a School Board Trustee, has a long record of public service in the region.

The impression left in many minds by such phrasings is that the person described as having a long record of public service is well suited to public office, while the person whose parenting is emphasised may be better suited to staying at home.

Some may feel that parenthood is relevant in such cases; if you do, be sure to mention it both for women and for men, and be sure to avoid unneccessary references to physical appearance. The general rule should be that parenting (and physical appearance) should not be mentioned unless you feel them relevant to the point(s) you are making.

6b. RACE, CULTURE, AND SEXUAL ORIENTATION

Although gender is the most contentious issue in the struggle for bias-free language, it is not the only one. Almost everyone is aware that one should avoid various terms for particular racial or cultural groups (see the list below), and it is just as important to avoid language that conveys derogatory implications on the basis of sexual orientation. The most appropriate terms to use do not stay constant, however; everything hinges on connotation, and since connotations may change over time, so does appropriate usage. The best principle to follow here is to pay attention to how members of particular groups prefer to be described.

A few racial and cultural terms are so deeply encoded in the language that people may use them without being aware of their underlying meaning.

offensive   I'm convinced that the shopkeeper tried to gyp me.
(*Gyp* originated in the prejudice that Roma were congenital cheats.)

bias-free   I'm convinced that the shopkeeper
tried to cheat me.

Another example of a widely-used expression that is strongly if more subtly coloured with bias is the expression *white trash*. The implications of the expression are brought forward in the following passage:

> The [Jerry Lee] Lewis and [Jimmy] Swaggart clans were, in the harsh modern parlance, white trash. They lived in the black part of town, and had close relations with blacks. Mr. Swaggart's preaching and Mr. Lewis's music were strongly influenced by black culture. "Jimmy Swaggart was as black as a white man can be," said black elders in Ferriday (*The Economist*, 15 April 2000).

This passage brings out the implication of the expression; the 'trashiness' that is the exception for white people is implicitly regarded as the norm for black people.

Given the generally high level of awareness in Western society of the evils of anti-Semitism, it is extraordinary that *jew* is still sometimes used in casual conversation as a verb in the same way that *gyp* is used. It is a use that should never be allowed to go unchallenged—and when such usages are challenged speakers will often realise they have been unthinkingly using a coinage learnt in childhood—and will change.

Less obviously offensive but still objectionable is the use of unnecessary racial or gender or religious identifiers. Mentioning a person's race or gender or religion in connection with occupation is a common habit, but one that reinforces stereotypes as to what sort of person one would naturally expect to be a lawyer or a doctor or a nurse. Unless race or gender or religion is in some way relevant to the conversation, there is no need to refer to someone as a *male nurse*, or a *Jewish doctor*, or a *Native lawyer*.

In one important respect the issue of bias-free usage differs from every other issue discussed in this book.

Throughout, our focus has been on formal writing, and it has frequently been emphasized that many informal and colloquial usages that are inappropriate to formal writing may be quite unexceptionable in other forms of writing, or in speech. The same cannot be said of the difference between biased and bias-free language. It is no less damaging to use sexist, racist, or homophobic language in speech than it is in writing; indeed, it may even be more so. The cumulative repetition in speech of colloquial expressions—including such 'innocent' expressions as the contemptuous use of "that's so gay"— probably does considerably more to reinforce human prejudice than does the written word.

6c. BIAS-FREE VOCABULARY: A SHORT LIST

actress	actor
alderman	councillor
Asiatic	Asian
bad guy	villain
bellboy	bellhop
bogeyman	bogey monster
businessman	businessperson, entrepreneur
caveman	cave-dweller
chairman	chair
clergyman	minister, member of the clergy
congressman	representative
con-man	con-artist
draftsman	drafter
Eskimo	Inuit

NB Some Alaskan groups still prefer *Eskimo*.

fireman	firefighter
fisherman	fisher
foreman	manager, supervisor
freshman	first-year student
garbageman	garbage collector
gunman	shooter
gyp	cheat, con
Gypsies	Roma
henchmen	thugs
Indian	Native, First Nations

NB As with Eskimo/Inuit and African American/Black, the key consideration is sensitivity to audience. If you do not belong to the group but you know that the people you are writing about prefer a particular designation, that is the one to use.

infantryman	foot soldier
layman	layperson
longshoreman	shiploader, stevedore
mailman	letter carrier, mail carrier
male nurse	nurse
man	humanity
man [an exhibit]	staff
man [a barricade]	fortify, occupy
man [a ship]	crew
manhandle	rough up, maul
manhole	sewer hole, access hole, street hole
manhole cover	sewer cover, street hole cover
mankind	human kind, people, humanity, humans
manly	self-confident, courageous, straightforward
man-made	handmade, constructed, synthetic
middleman	intermediary
negro	black, African American

NB In the United States *African American* is generally preferred; in Canada *black* is often the preferred term.

niggardly	stingy

NB The word *niggardly* has no etymological connection with *nigger*. Since the one suggests the other to many minds, however, it is safer to avoid using it.

Oriental	Asian, Middle Eastern
policeman	police officer
postman	letter carrier, mail carrier
salesman	salesperson
snowman	snowbody (rhymes with *nobody*)
sportsman	sportsperson
stewardess	flight attendant
unsportsmanlike	unsporting
weatherman	weather forecaster
womanly	warm, tender, nurturing, sympathetic
workman	worker, labourer

ON THE WEB

Exercises on bias-free language may be found at
www.broadviewpress.com/writing.
Click on **Exercises** and go to **D53–D54**.

GRAMMAR

7. VERBS AND VERB TENSE DIFFICULTIES

7a. THE INFINITIVE

The infinitive is the starting point for building a knowledge of verb tenses; it is the most basic form of the verb. Some examples of infinitives are *to go, to be, to do, to begin, to come, to investigate*. The infinitive form remains the same whether the action referred to happens in the past, the present, or the future.

The most commonly made mistake involving infinitives is the colloquial substitution of *and* for *to*, especially in the expression *try and do it* for *try to do it*. The great issue in this area among grammarians, however, is the **split infinitive**—the infinitive which has another word or words inserted between *to* and the verb: *to quickly go; to forcefully speak out; to thoroughly investigate*. Some authorities argue that it is always grammatically incorrect to break up the infinitive in this way. Most, however, see the matter as one of awkwardness rather than incorrectness. In most cases a sentence with a split infinitive will sound more awkward than one without—but this is not a firm and fast rule.

7b. THE SIMPLE PRESENT TENSE

	SINGULAR	PLURAL
1st person	I say	we say
2nd person	you say	you say
3rd person	he, she, it says	they say

7c. SUBJECT-VERB AGREEMENT

Almost all of us occasionally have problems in writing the third person of the simple present tense correctly. All too often the letter *s* at the end of the third person singular is left out. The simple rule here is that whenever you use a verb in the third person singular of the simple present tense, it *must* end in *s*.

needs checking	The compound change shape when heated.
revised	The compound changes shape when heated. (*Compound*, which is the subject, is an *it* and therefore third person singular.)

It is not particularly difficult to make the subject agree with the verb in the above example. Even professional writers often have trouble with more complex sentences. Two common causes of subject-verb agreement errors are discussed below.

a) The subject and verb are separated by a long phrase or clause*

needs checking	The recent history of these African nations illustrate a variety of points.
revised	The recent history of these African nations illustrates a variety of points.

Here the writer has made the mental error of thinking of *nations* as the subject of the verb *illustrate*, whereas in fact the subject is the singular noun *history*. "The history illustrate..." would immediately strike most people as wrong, but the intervening words have in this case caused grammatical confusion.

needs checking	As the statement by Belgium's Prime Minister about his country's deficit and unemployment problems indicate, many nations are in the same shape, or worse.
revised	As the statement by Belgium's Prime Minister about his country's deficit and unemployment problems indicates, many nations are in the same shape, or worse. (The subject is the singular noun *statement*, so the verb must be *indicates* rather than *indicate*.)

*See the Reference Guide to Basic Grammar at the back of the book for a discussion of phrases and clauses.

b) The error of using *there is* instead of *there are* when the subject is plural has become more and more frequent in writing as well as speech. When these two expressions are used, remember that the subject comes <u>after</u> the verb; use *is* or *are* depending on whether the subject is singular or plural.

needs checking	There's more people here than there were last year.
revised	There are more people here than there were last year.

7d. SURVEY OF VERB TENSES

1ˢᵗ PERSON:

the present progressive (or continuous) tense	I am finishing
the simple past tense	I finished
the past progressive (or continuous) tense	I was finishing
the simple future tense	I will finish
the future progressive (or continuous) tense	I will be finishing
the present perfect tense	I have finished
the past perfect tense	I had finished
the future perfect tense	I will have finished
the conditional	I would finish
the past conditional	I would have finished
the present perfect continuous	I have been finishing
the past perfect continuous	I had been finishing
the future perfect continuous	I will have been finishing
the conditional continuous	I would be finishing
the past conditional continuous	I would have been finishing

7e. VOICE

Most verbs have both an **active** and a **passive** voice. The active is used when the subject of the verb is doing the action, whereas the passive is used when the subject of the verb is receiving the action or being acted *on*. Some examples:

ACTIVE	PASSIVE
I did it.	It was done.
She hit him.	He was hit.
They will give a speech.	The speech will be given.

Mood: Most sentences in English are in the *indicative mood*, which is used when we are expressing facts and opinions or asking questions. We use the *imperative mood* when giving orders or advice, and we use the *subjunctive mood* to denote actions that are wished for or.imagined, or would happen if certain conditions were met. Some examples:

> If I were you, I would do what she says.
> The doctor advises that he stop smoking immediately.
> (not *that he stops*)

needs checking	If a bank was willing to lend money without proper guarantees, it would go bankrupt very quickly.
revised	If a bank were willing to lend money without proper guarantees, it would go bankrupt very quickly.

For more on conditions see pages 58–59.

8. COMBINING VERB TENSES

8a. THE PAST PERFECT TENSE

The chief use of the past perfect tense is to show that one action in the past was completed before another action in the past began:

> I told my parents what <u>had happened</u>.
> (The happening occurred before the telling.)

> She thought very seriously about what he <u>had said</u>.
> (The saying occurred before the thinking.)

The past perfect is particularly useful when the writer wishes to flashback, or move backwards in time:

needs checking	The tail was still moving, but the snake itself was quite dead. It crawled out from under a rock and slowly moved towards me as I was lowering the canoe at the end of the portage.
revised	The tail was still moving, but the snake itself was quite dead. It had crawled out from under a rock and had moved slowly towards me as I had been lowering the canoe at the end of the portage.

The past perfect is frequently used when we are reporting speech indirectly:

She said that she <u>had finished</u> the work, and we asked him when he <u>had known</u> of the diversion of funds.

8b. COMBINING TENSES—QUOTED MATERIAL

It is often difficult to achieve grammatical consistency when incorporating quoted material in a sentence:

needs checking	Prime Minister Wilson admitted at the time that "such a policy is not without its drawbacks."
	(The past tense *admitted* and the present tense *is* do not agree.)

There are two ways of dealing with a difficulty such as this:

(a) Change the sentence so as to set off the quotation without using the connecting word *that*. Usually this can be done with a colon.

(b) Use only that part of the quotation that can be used in such a way as to agree with the tense of the main verb.

revised	Prime Minister Wilson did not claim perfection: "such a policy is not without its drawbacks," he admitted.

or   Prime Minister Wilson admitted at the time that such a policy was "not without its drawbacks."

9. IRREGULAR VERBS

The majority of verbs in English follow a regular pattern—I *open* in the simple present tense, I *opened* in the simple past tense, I *have opened* in the present perfect tense, and so forth. Most of the more frequently used verbs, however, follow different patterns. For example, we say *I went* instead of *I goed*. Here is a list of irregular verbs in English:

BASE FORM	SIMPLE PAST	PAST PARTICIPLE
arise	arose	arisen
awake	awoke/awaked	awoken/awaked/woken
be	was/were	been
bear	bore	borne
beat	beat	beaten
become	became	become
begin	began	begun
bend	bent	bent
bite	bit	bitten
bleed	bled	bled
blow	blew	blown
break	broke	broken
bring	brought	brought
build	built	built
burn	burned/burnt	burned/burnt
burst	burst	burst
buy	bought	bought
can	could	been able
catch	caught	caught
choose	chose	chosen
cling	clung	clung
come	came	come
dig	dug	dug
do	did	done
dive	dived/dove	dived

drag	dragged	dragged
draw	drew	drawn
dream	dreamed/dreamt	dreamed/dreamt
drink	drank	drunk
drive	drove	driven
eat	ate	eaten
fall	fell	fallen
feel	felt	felt
fight	fought	fought
find	found	found
fit	fitted or fit (US)	fitted
flee	fled	fled
fling	flung	flung
fly	flew	flown
forbid	forbade	forbidden
forecast	forecast	forecast
forget	forgot	forgotten
forgive	forgave	forgiven
freeze	froze	frozen
get	got	got
give	gave	given
go	went	gone
grind	ground	ground
grow	grew	grown
hang	hanged/hung	hanged/hung
have	had	had
hear	heard	heard
hide	hid	hidden
hold	held	held
hurt	hurt	hurt
keep	kept	kept
kneel	knelt	knelt
know	knew	known
lay	laid	laid
lead	led	led
lean	leaned/leant	leaned/leant
leap	leaped/leapt	leaped/leapt
learn	learned/learnt	learned/learnt
leave	left	left
lend	lent	lent
let	let	let
lie	lay	lain
light	lighted/lit	lighted/lit

lose	lost	lost
make	made	made
may	might	
mean	meant	meant
meet	met	met
must	had to	had to
pay	paid	paid
prove	proved	proven/proved
put	put	put
read	read	read
ride	rode	ridden
ring	rang	rung
rise	rose	risen
run	ran	run
saw	sawed	sawed/sawn
say	said	said
see	saw	seen
seek	sought	sought
sell	sold	sold
sew	sewed	sewed/sewn
shake	shook	shaken
shall	should	
shine	shone	shone
shoot	shot	shot
show	showed	showed/shown
shrink	shrank	shrunk
shut	shut	shut
sing	sang	sung
sink	sank	sunk
sit	sat	sat
sleep	slept	slept
smell	smelled/smelt	smelled/smelt
sow	sowed	sowed/sown
speak	spoke	spoken
speed	speeded/sped	speeded/sped
spell	spelled/spelt	spelled/spelt
spend	spent	spent
spill	spilled/spilt	spilled/spilt
spin	spun	spun
spit	spat	spat
split	split	split
spread	spread	spread
spring	sprang	sprung

stand	stood	stood
steal	stole	stolen
stick	struck	stuck
sting	stung	stung
strike	struck	struck
swear	swore	sworn
sweep	swept	swept
swim	swam	swum
swing	swung	swung
teach	taught	taught
tear	tore	torn
tell	told	told
think	thought	thought
throw	threw	thrown
tread	trod	trodden/trod
understand	understood	understood
wake	waked/woke	waked/woken
wear	wore	worn
weep	wept	wept
win	won	won
wind	wound	wound
wring	wrung	wrung
write	wrote	written

needs checking   A problem had arose even before the discussion began.

revised   A problem had arisen even before the discussion began.

needs checking   In 1948 Newfoundlanders choose to join Canada.

revised   In 1948 Newfoundlanders chose to join Canada.

needs checking   Thucydides analized the events that lead to the Peloponnesian war.

revised   Thucydides analized the events that led to the Peloponnesian war.

needs checking   The report laid on her desk until Thursday afternoon.

revised   The report lay on her desk until Thursday afternoon.

needs checking	The government's majority shrunk in the election.
revised	The government's majority shrank in the election.
needs checking	Pictures were taken while the royal couple swum in what they had thought was a private cove.
revised	Pictures were taken while the royal couple swam in what they had thought was a private cove.

10. DANGLING CONSTRUCTIONS

Participles, infinitives, and gerunds may all be used to introduce phrases within sentences. With phrases of this sort, it is important to make sure that the participle, infinitive, or gerund relates grammatically to the subject of the adjacent main clause.

needs checking	Waiting for a bus, a brick fell on my head. (Bricks do not normally wait for buses.)
revised	While I was waiting for a bus, a brick fell on my head.

In sentences such as this one the absurdity is easy to notice; it is much more difficult to do so with longer and more complex sentences.

needs checking	Considering all the above-mentioned studies, the evidence shows conclusively that smoking can cause cancer.
revised	Considering all the above-mentioned studies, we conclude that smoking causes cancer.
better	These studies show conclusively that smoking can cause cancer.
needs checking	Turning for a moment to the thorny question of Joyce's style, the stream of

	consciousness technique realistically depicts the workings of the human mind. (The stream should not be doing the turning.)
revised	Turning for a moment to the thorny question of Joyce's style, we may observe that his stream of consciousness technique realistically depicts the workings of the human mind.
better	Joyce's style does not make *Ulysses* easy to read, but his stream of consciousness technique realistically depicts the workings of the human mind.
needs checking	Considered from a cost point of view, Combo Capital Corporation could not really afford to purchase Skinflint Securities. (Combo is not being considered; the purchase is.)
revised	Considered from the point of view of cost, the purchase of Skinflint Securities was not a wise move by Combo Capital Corporation.
better	Combo Capital Corporation could not really afford to buy Skinflint Securities.
needs checking	Once regarded as daringly modern in its portrayal of fashionable *fin de siècle* decadence, Wilde draws on traditional patterns to create a powerful Gothic tale. (The novel is an "it"; Oscar Wilde was a "he.")
revised	*The Picture of Dorian Gray* was once regarded as daringly modern in its portrayal of fashionable *fin de siècle* decadence. In the novel Wilde draws on traditional patterns to create a powerful Gothic tale.
needs checking	To conclude this essay, the French Revolution was a product of many interacting causes. (The French Revolution concluded no essays.)

poor	To conclude this essay, let me say that the French Revolution was a product of many causes.
better	The explanations given for the French Revolution, then, are not mutually exclusive; it was a product of many interacting causes.

needs checking	In reviewing the evidence, one point stands out plainly.
	(A point cannot review evidence.)
poor	In reviewing the evidence, we can see one point standing out plainly.
better	One point stands out plainly from this evidence.

Notice that the best way to eliminate the problem of dangling constructions is often to dispense with the original phrase entirely.

11. NOUNS AND PRONOUNS

(See also pages 70–71.)

Nouns are words that name people, things, places, or qualities. The following words are all nouns: *boy, John, spaghetti, Zambia, silence, anger.*

Pronouns replace or stand for nouns. For example, instead of saying "The man slipped on a banana peel" or "George slipped on a banana peel," we can replace the noun *man* (or the noun *George*) with the pronoun *he* and say "He slipped on a banana peel." A discussion of some problems commonly experienced with nouns and pronouns follows.

ON THE WEB

Exercises on dangling constructions and on nouns and pronouns may be found at

www.broadviewpress.com/writing.

Click on **Exercises** and go to **A13–A16** and to **A149–A179**.

11a. SINGULAR AND PLURAL NOUNS

Some nouns are unusual in the way that a plural is formed.
Here is a list of some that frequently cause mistakes:

appendix	appendixes or appendices
attorney general	attorneys general
bacterium	bacteria
basis	bases
court martial	courts martial
crisis	crises
criterion	criteria
curriculum	curricula
datum	data
ellipsis	ellipses
emphasis	emphases
erratum	errata
father-in-law	fathers-in-law
focus	focuses or foci
governor general	governors general
index	indexes or indices
matrix	matrixes or matrices
medium	media
millennium	millennia
nucleus	nuclei
parenthesis	parentheses
phenomenon	phenomena
referendum	referenda or referendums
runner-up	runners-up
stratum	strata
symposium	symposia
synthesis	syntheses
thesis	theses

needs checking	The chief criteria on which an essay should be judged is whether or not it communicates clearly.
revised	The chief criterion on which an essay should be judged is whether or not it communicates clearly.
needs checking	This data proves conclusively that the lake is badly polluted.

revised	These data prove conclusively that the lake is badly polluted.
needs checking	The media usually assumes that the audience has a very short attention span.
revised	The media usually assume that the audience has a very short attention span.
needs checking	The great popularity of 'beanie babies' was a short-lived phenomena.
revised	The great popularity of 'beanie babies' was a short-lived phenomenon.

11b. SINGULAR PRONOUNS

The pronouns *anybody, anyone, each, each other, either, every, neither, nobody, no one, one another* are all singular. In order to be grammatically correct, they should therefore take singular verbs.

needs checking	According to a poll of the electorate and the party, neither seem satisfied with the leader's performance.
revised	According to a poll of the electorate and the party, neither seems satisfied with the leader's performance.

The particular case of balancing grammatical agreements, syntactical awkwardness, and issues of gender is dealt with elsewhere in this book under **bias-free language**, pages 27–29.

11c. UNREFERENCED OR WRONGLY REFERENCED PRONOUNS

Normally a pronoun must refer to a noun in the previous sentence or clause.

needs checking	A herbalist knows a lot about the properties of plants. They can often cure you by giving you medicine.

revised	A herbalist knows a lot about the properties of plants. He can often cure you by giving you medicine.
better	Herbalists know a lot about the properties of plants. They can often cure you by giving you medicine.

Confusion can result if there is more than one possible referent for a pronoun.

needs checking	My father and my brother visited me early this morning. He told me that something important had happened.
revised	My father and my brother visited me early this morning. My father told me that something important had happened.

needs checking	The deficit was forecast to be $2 billion, but turned out to be over $20 billion. This reflected the government's failure to predict the increase in interest rates and the onset of a recession. (This *what* ?)
revised	The deficit was forecast to be $2 billion, but turned out to be over $20 billion. This vast discrepancy reflected the government's failure to predict the increase in interest rates and the onset of a recession.

11d. SUBJECT AND OBJECT PRONOUNS

Different forms of certain pronouns are used depending on whether we are using them as a subject or an object. *I, we, he/she/it, they,* and *who* are subject pronouns, whereas *me, us, him/her/it, them,* and *whom* are object pronouns.

He shot the sheriff.

(Here the pronoun *he* is the subject of the sentence.)

The sheriff shot him.
(Here the word *him* is the object; the *sheriff* is the subject.)

That is the man who shot the sheriff.
(Here the pronoun *who* is the subject of the clause *who shot the sheriff*.)

That is the man whom the sheriff shot.
(Here the pronoun *whom* is the object; the *sheriff* shot.)

Perhaps as a result of the slang use of *me* as a subject pronoun ("Me and him got together for a few beer last night"), the impression seems to have lodged in many minds that the distinction between **I** and **me** is one of degree of politeness or formality rather than one of subject and object.

needs checking	There is no disagreement between you and I.
revised	There is no disagreement between you and me.

(Both *you* and *I* are here objects of the preposition *between*. "Between you and I" is no more correct than is "I threw the ball at he.")

Though the grammatical distinction between **who** and **whom** is in theory just as clear as the distinction between *I* and *me* or the distinction between *she* and *her*, in common usage it is much more blurred. The subject-object distinction in this case has largely broken down; the grammatically correct form often sounds awkward, and many authorities no longer insist on the distinction always being maintained. For example, even grammatical purists sometimes find themselves saying "I didn't know who I was talking to," even though the rules say it should be *whom* (subject—*I*; object—*to whom*).

12. ADJECTIVES AND ADVERBS

Adjectives are words used to tell us more about (*describe* or *modify*) nouns or pronouns. *Big, small, good, careful,* and *expensive* are all examples of adjectives. Adverbs

are usually used to tell us more about (*describe* or *modify*) verbs, although they can also be used to modify adjectives or other adverbs. *Carefully, expensively, suddenly,* and *slowly* are all examples of adverbs. In conversation adjectives are often substituted for certain adverbs, but this should not be done in formal writing.

needs checking	She did good on the test.
revised	She did well on the test.

needs checking	He asked them not to talk so loud.
revised	He asked them not to talk so loudly.

needs checking	The governors thought it should be worded different.
revised	The governors thought it should be worded differently.

needs checking	They promised to do the job cheaper, easier, and quicker.
revised	They promised to do the job more cheaply, more easily, and more quickly.

12a. COMPARATIVES AND SUPERLATIVES

Most adjectives and adverbs have comparative and superlative forms; the comparative is used when comparing two things, the superlative when comparing three or more.

needs checking	Smith was the most accomplished of the two.
revised	Smith was the more accomplished of the two.

Always be careful not to construct double comparisons:

needs checking	Gandalf is much more wiser than Frodo.
revised	Gandalf is much wiser than Frodo.

13. SENTENCE FRAGMENTS/ INCOMPLETE SENTENCES

Even those with little formal knowledge of the distinction between main clauses and subordinate clauses generally understand that the group of words "Marina walked to the sea" is a complete sentence, whereas the group of words "When Marina walked to the sea" does not form a grammatically complete sentence. Interestingly, the longer a subordinate clause becomes, the more difficult it may be to recognize that it still does not form a complete sentence:

needs checking   While Marina was walking to the sea and thinking of her father and the sound of a wood thrush.

revised   While Marina was walking to the sea, she heard the sound of a wood thrush and thought of her father.

needs checking   So long as you have a place to live, and enough to eat, and loved ones nearby.

revised   So long as you have a place to live, and enough to eat, and loved ones nearby, you have reason to be thankful.

Incomplete sentences frequently involve the words *because* and *whereas*. Whenever you use *because* in a sentence the sentence must mention <u>both</u> the cause and the result. Whether the word *because* comes at the beginning or in the middle of the sentence does not matter; what is important is that the sentence have two parts.

needs checking   In the early 1980s Sandinista leaders told their people to be ready for war. Because the United States had been trying to destabilize Nicaragua.

revised   In the early 1980s Sandinista leaders told their people to be ready for war,

> because the United States had been
> trying to destabilize Nicaragua.

Whereas should be used to join ideas together into one sentence:

needs checking   This artist's recent paintings are mostly abstract. Whereas her earlier work is rendered quite realistically.

revised   This artist's recent paintings are mostly abstract, whereas her earlier work is rendered quite realistically.

When writing informally, experienced writers sometimes intentionally write sentences that are grammatically incomplete. Normally this is done as a means of adding emphasis:

> In the end she was convinced that this was the best way. The only way.

> At first the police believed it to be a simple case of mistaken identity. But not for long.

14. RUN-ON SENTENCES/COMMA SPLICES

The basic idea that groups of words containing complete, separate ideas cannot be made into one sentence unless one employs an appropriate joining word or a semi-colon is quite straightforward.

needs checking   Early last Thursday we were walking in the woods, it was a bright and clear morning.

revised   Early last Thursday we were walking in the woods. It was a bright and clear morning.

The conventions of English dictate that words classed as coordinating conjunctions may be used to join independent clauses into a single sentence. Words that are commonly used in this way include *and, but, for, nor, or, so,* and *yet.*

Another class of joining words is the conjunctive adverb. Some of the words most commonly used as conjunctive adverbs are *also, hence, however, moreover, nevertheless, otherwise*, and *therefore*. When used as conjunctive adverbs, these words typically indicate how the main idea in one sentence relates to the main idea of a previous sentence. In such cases a period (or a semi-colon) should separate the ideas from each other. They should not be "spliced" together by a comma:

needs checking	During the rainy season more water flows over Victoria Falls than over any other falls in the world, however several other falls are higher than Victoria.
revised	During the rainy season more water flows over Victoria Falls than over any other falls in the world. However, several other falls are higher than Victoria.
needs checking	Technology is perceived to be good for the economy and society, companies are therefore often able to persuade governments to subsidize their efforts to develop new technology.
revised	Technology is perceived to be good for the economy and society; therefore companies are often able to persuade governments to subsidize their efforts to develop new technology.

Unlike *when, then* should not be used to join two clauses together into a single sentence. *And then* may be used, or a semi-colon, or a new sentence may be begun.

needs checking	We applied the solution to the surface of the leaves, then we made observations at half hour intervals over the next twelve hours.
revised	We applied the solution to the surface of the leaves, and then we made

observations at half hour intervals over the next twelve hours.

ON THE WEB

Exercises on sentence fragments, on comma splices, and for those whose native language is not English may be found at

www.broadviewpress.com/writing.

Click on **Exercises** and go to **F1–F7** and to **E1–E18**.

15. FOR THOSE WHOSE NATIVE LANGUAGE IS NOT ENGLISH

The fact that different languages have different grammatical and syntactical conventions creates particular problems for anyone learning a new language. This section focuses on some of the peculiarities of English that are particularly likely to present difficulties to those learning the language.

15a. ARTICLES

Articles are words used to introduce nouns. Unlike many other languages, English often requires the use of articles:

needs checking   We are interested in house with garage.
revised   We are interested in a house with a garage.

There are only three articles—*a, an,* and *the.* Articles show whether or not one is drawing attention to a <u>particular</u> person or thing. For example, we would say "I stood beside a house" if we did not want to draw attention to that particular house, but "I stood beside the house that the Taylors used to live in" if we wanted to draw attention to the particular house.

A (or *an* if the noun following begins with a vowel sound) is an <u>indefinite</u> article—used when you do not

want to be definite or specific about which thing or person you are referring to. *The* is a <u>definite</u> article, used when you do wish to call attention to the particular thing or person. Remember that if you use *the* you are suggesting that there can be only <u>one</u> of what you are referring to.

In order to use articles properly in English it is important to understand the distinction English makes between nouns naming things that are countable (*houses, books, trees,* etc.) and nouns naming things that are not countable (*milk, confusion,* etc.). Some non-count nouns name things that it does seem possible to count: *sugar, grass, furniture,* etc. In such cases counting must in English be done indirectly: *a grain of sugar, two grains of sugar, three blades of grass, four pieces of furniture,* and so on.

Distinguishing between count and non-count nouns is inevitably a challenge for those whose first language is not English. A dictionary such as *The Oxford Advanced Learner's Dictionary* can be very helpful; unlike most dictionaries it indicates whether or not each noun is a count noun.

needs checking	They bought a nice furniture for the living room.
revised	They bought a nice piece of furniture for the living room.

15b. FREQUENTLY USED NON-COUNT NOUNS

Abstractions: advice, anger, beauty, confidence, courage, employment, fun, happiness, hate, health, honesty, information, intelligence, knowledge, love, poverty, truth, wealth, wisdom.

To eat and drink: bacon, beef, beer, bread, broccoli, butter, cabbage, candy, cauliflower, celery, cereal, cheese, chicken, chocolate, coffee, corn, cream, fish, flour, fruit, ice, ice cream, lettuce, margarine, meat, milk, oil, pasta, pepper, rice, salt, spinach, sugar, tea, water, wine, yogurt.

Other substances, things, and actions: air, cement, clothing, coal, dirt, equipment, furniture, gas, gasoline, gold, grass, homework, jewelry, luggage, lumber, machinery, metal, mail, money, music, paper, petroleum, plastic, poetry, pollution, research, scenery, silver, snow, soap, steel, timber, traffic, transportation, violence, weather, wood, wool, work.

NB The plural of many of these non-count nouns may be employed when you want to denote more than one *type* of the substance. *Breads*, for example, refers to different sorts of bread; *coffees* refers to different types of coffee, and so on.

Articles are not used in English to the same extent that they are used in some other languages; nouns can frequently stand alone without their article, particularly when they are being used in a general, non-specific sense. When used in this way, non-count and plural-count nouns need no article.

needs checking	If the English is to be spoken correctly, the good grammar is important.
revised	If English is to be spoken correctly, good grammar is important.

needs checking	The freedom is something everyone values.
revised	Freedom is something everyone values.

In most cases no article is necessary before a noun that is capitalized:

needs checking	They were strolling through the Stanley Park.
revised	They were strolling through Stanley Park.

15c. CONTINUOUS VERB TENSES

In English the continuous tenses are not normally used with many verbs having to do with feelings, emotions, or senses. Some of these verbs are *to see, to hear, to understand, to believe, to hope, to know, to think* (meaning *believe*), *to trust, to comprehend, to mean, to doubt, to suppose, to wish, to want, to love, to desire, to prefer, to dislike, to hate.*

needs checking	He is not understanding what I mean.
revised	He does not understand what I mean.

needs checking	At that time he was believing that everything on Earth was created within one week.
revised	At that time he believed that everything on Earth was created within one week.

15d. OMISSION OR REPETITION OF THE SUBJECT

With the exception of imperatives (e.g. *Come here! Don't stop!*), where *you* is understood to be the subject, English requires that the subject of the sentence be stated. Some other languages permit the omission of the subject in various circumstances where the subject may be inferred. English does not.

needs checking	The protesters demonstrated peacefully; stood quietly outside the gates of the Prime Minister's residence.
revised	The protesters demonstrated peacefully; they stood quietly outside the gates of the Prime Minister's residence.

If the subject appears after the verb, a frequent requirement in English is for *there* or *it* to be added as an expletive before the verb *to be.*

needs checking	Is not possible to finish the job this week.

revised	It is not possible to finish the job this week.
needs checking	By the end of the century, were almost one million more people in Houston than there had been in 1980.
revised	By the end of the century, there were almost one million more people in Houston than there had been in 1980.

Within a single clause English does not permit the repetition of either the subject or the object.

needs checking	The line that is longest it is called the hypotenuse.
revised	The line that is longest is called the hypotenuse.
needs checking	The members of the cast loved the play that they were acting in it.
revised	The members of the cast loved the play that they were acting in.

15e. THE CONDITIONAL

Particular rules apply in English when we are speaking of actions which *would happen if* certain conditions were fulfilled. Here are some examples.

If I *went* to Australia, I *would have* to fly.

If I *drank* a lot of gin, I *would be* very sick.

I *would lend* Joe the money he wants if I *trusted* him.

Each of these sentences is made up of a main clause in which the conditional *would have, would be,* etc. is used, and a subordinate clause beginning with *if*, with a verb

in the simple past tense (*went, drank, trusted*). In all cases the action named in the *if* clause is considered by the speaker to be unlikely to happen, or quite impossible. The first speaker does not really think that she will go to Australia; she is just speculating about what would be necessary if she did go. Similarly, the second speaker does not expect to drink a lot of gin, and the third speaker does not trust Joe. Situations like these, which are not happening and which we do not expect to happen are called *hypothetical situations*; we speculate on what *would* happen *if* but we do not expect the *if* to come true.

If we think the *if* is indeed likely to come true, then we use the future tense instead of the conditional in the main clause, and the present tense in the subordinate *if* clause, as in these examples:

If I drink a lot of gin I will be very sick.
(The speaker thinks it quite possible that he will drink a lot of gin.)

If I go to Australia, I will have to fly.
(The speaker thinks that she may really go.)

Some writers mistakenly use the conditional or the present tense (instead of the past tense form) in the *if* clause when they are using the conditional in the main clause:

needs checking	If I want to buy a car, I would look carefully at all the models available.
revised	If I wanted to buy a car, I would look carefully at all the models available. (The speaker does not want to buy a car.)
or	If I want to buy a car, I will look carefully at all the models available. (The speaker may really want to buy a car.)
needs checking	If the authorities would find out what happened, both boys would be in serious trouble.

revised	If the authorities found out what happened, both boys would be in serious trouble.
or	If the authorities were to find out what happened, both boys would be in serious trouble.

Similar problems occur with the past conditional:

needs checking	If the Titanic would have carried more lifeboats, hundreds of lives would have been saved.
revised	If the Titanic had carried more lifeboats, hundreds of lives would have been saved.

ON THE WEB

Exercises on the conditional may be found at
www.broadviewpress.com/writing.
Click on **Exercises** and go to **A11**.

PUNCTUATION

16. THE PERIOD

The period (or full stop) is used to close sentences that make statements. Common difficulties with run-on sentences and incomplete sentences are discussed above in the section on grammar.

Notice that when a question is reported in indirect speech it has the form of a statement, and the sentence should therefore be closed with a period:

needs checking   He asked what time it was?
revised   He asked what time it was.

The period is also used to form abbreviations (*Mr., Ms., Hon., Ph.D., A.M., P.M., Inc.,* etc.). If you are in any doubt about whether or not to use a period in an abbreviation, or where to put it, think of the full form of what is being abbreviated.

needs checking   Jones, Smithers, et. al. will be there in person.
    (*et al. is short for the Latin et alia, "and others."*)
revised   Jones, Smithers, et al. will be there in person.

17. THE COMMA

The comma is used to indicate pauses, and to give the reader cues as to how the parts of the sentence relate to one another.

needs checking   Because of the work that we had done before we were ready to hand in the assignment.
revised   Because of the work that we had done before, we were ready to hand in the assignment.

The omission or addition of a comma can completely alter the meaning of a sentence—as it did in the Queen's University Alumni letter that spoke of the warm emotions still felt by alumni for "our friends, who are dead."

17a. EXTRA COMMA

Commas should follow the grammatical structure of a sentence; you should not throw in a comma simply because a sentence is getting long.

needs checking   The ever increasing gravitational pull of the global economy, is drawing almost every area of the earth into its orbit.

revised   The ever increasing gravitational pull of the global economy is drawing almost every area of the earth into its orbit.

17b. COMMAS AND LISTS

An important use of commas is to separate the entries in lists. Some authorities feel that a comma need not appear between the last and second last entries in a list, since these are usually separated already by the word *and*. Omitting the last comma in a series, however, will occasionally lead to ambiguity. When in doubt, it is always best to include the serial comma.

needs checking   The book is dedicated to my parents, Ayn Rand and God.

revised   The book is dedicated to my parents, Ayn Rand, and God.

When a list includes items that have commas within them, use a semi-colon to separate the items in the list.

needs checking   The three firms involved were McCarthy and Walters, Harris, Jones, and Engelby, and Cassells and Wirtz.

revised   The three firms involved were
                             McCarthy and Walters; Harris, Jones,
                             and Engelby; and Cassells and Wirtz.

17c. COMMAS AND NON-RESTRICTIVE ELEMENTS

There is a significant difference of meaning between the
following two sentences:

The dancers who wore black looked very elegant.

The dancers, who wore black, looked very elegant.

In the first sentence, the words *who wore black* restrict
the meaning of the noun *dancers*; the implication is that
also present were dancers not wearing black, and
perhaps looking rather less elegant. In the second
sentence the words *who wore black* are set off in
commas. This signifies that they do not act to restrict the
meaning of the noun *dancers*. Instead, they add
information that must be assumed to apply to the entire
group; we infer that *all* the dancers wore black.

One important use of commas, then, is to set off
non-restrictive elements of sentences:

restrictive   A company that pays no attention to
                             its customers is unlikely to survive.
non-restrictive   The local grocery, which is always
                             attentive to its customers, has been a
                             fixture for generations.

restrictive   The man with abdominal pains was
                             treated before any of the others.
non-restrictive   Mr. Smith, who suffered from abdominal
                             pains, was treated before the others.

restrictive   The film *Chinatown* is in many ways
                             reminiscent of films of the 1950s.
non-restrictive   Polanski's seventh film in English,
                             Chinatown, is regarded by many as the
                             finest film ever made.

Notice that the commas here come in pairs. If a non-restrictive element is being set off in the middle of a sentence, it must be set off on both sides.

needs checking	My sister Caroline, has done very well this year in her studies.
revised	My sister, Caroline, has done very well this year in her studies.
needs checking	The snake which had been killed the day before, was already half-eaten by ants.
revised	The snake, which had been killed the day before, was already half-eaten by ants.

17d. THAT AND *WHICH*

It is correct to use *that* in restrictive clauses and *which* in non-restrictive clauses.

needs checking	The only store which sells this brand is now closed.
revised	The only store that sells this brand is now closed.
needs checking	The position which Marx adopted owed much to the philosophy of Hegel.
revised	The position that Marx adopted owed much to the philosophy of Hegel.

Although the use of the word *which* in any restrictive clause provokes a violent reaction among some English instructors, there are some instances in which one is quite justified in using *which* in this way. Such is the case when the writer is already using at least one *that* in the sentence:

needs checking	He told me that the radio that he had bought was defective.
revised	He told me that the radio which he had bought was defective.

18. THE QUESTION MARK

Any direct question should be followed by a question mark.

needs checking	Would Britain benefit from closer ties with Europe. More than thirty years after the UK joined the EC, the question continues to bedevil British political life.
revised	Would Britain benefit from closer ties with Europe? More than thirty years after the UK joined the EC, the question continues to bedevil British political life.

If a polite request is couched as a question, a question mark is appropriate.

needs checking	Would you please make sure the pages are in proper order.
revised	Would you please make sure the pages are in proper order?

19. THE EXCLAMATION MARK

This mark is used to give extremely strong emphasis to a statement or a command. It is often used in personal or business correspondence, but it should be used very sparingly, if at all, in formal written work.

20. THE SEMI-COLON

The chief use of the semi-colon is to separate independent clauses whose ideas are closely related to each other. In most such cases a period could be used instead; the semi-colon simply signals to the reader the close relationship between the two ideas.

correct	The team is not as good as it used to be. It has lost four of its five last games.
also correct	The team is not as good as it used to be; it has lost four of its five last games.

As discussed elsewhere in this book (in the context of **joining ideas** and of **run-on sentences**) the semi-colon may often be used to correct a comma splice.

The semi-colon is also used to divide items in a series that includes other punctuation:

> The following were told to report to the coach after practice: Jackson, Form 2B; Marshall, Form 3A; Jones, Form 1B.

21. THE COLON

This mark is often believed to be virtually the same as the semi-colon in the way it is used. In fact, there are some important differences. The most common uses of the colon are as follows:

- in headings or titles to announce that more is to follow, or that the writer is about to list a series of things
- after an independent clause to introduce a quotation
- after an independent clause to indicate that what follows provides an explanation

This last use is very similar to the main use of the semi-colon. The subtle differences are that the semi-colon can be used in such situations when the ideas are not quite so closely related, and the colon asks the reader to pause for a slightly longer period. Here are some examples:

> Unquiet Union: A Study of the Federation of Rhodesia and Nyasaland.

> In the last four weeks he has visited five different countries: Mexico, Venezuela, Panama, Haiti, and Belize.

> The theory of the Communists may be summed up
> in the single phrase: abolition of private property.

Be sure to use a colon to introduce a list.

needs checking	The dealership has supplied Mr. Bomersbach with four luxury cars, two Cadillacs, a Mercedes, and a Jaguar.
revised	The dealership has supplied Mr. Bomersbach with four luxury cars: two Cadillacs, a Mercedes, and a Jaguar.

22. THE HYPHEN

This mark may be used to separate two parts of a
compound word (e.g., *tax-free, hand-operated*). Notice
that many such combinations are only hyphenated when
they are acting as an adjective:

> No change is planned for the short term.
> (*Term* here acts as a noun, with the adjective *short* modifying it.)

> This is only a short-term plan.
> (Here the compound *short-term* acts as a single adjective, modifying
> the noun *plan*.)

> The course will cover the full range of nineteenth-
> century literature.
> (Here the compound *nineteenth-century* acts as a single adjective,
> modifying the noun *literature*.)

> The course will cover the full scope of literature in
> the nineteenth century.
> (*Century* acts here as a noun, with the adjective *nineteenth*
> modifying it.)

Hyphens are also used to break up words at the end of
a line. When they are used in this way, hyphens should
always be placed between syllables. Proper nouns (i.e.,

nouns beginning with a capital letter) should not be broken up by hyphens.

23. THE DASH

Dashes are often used in much the same way as parentheses, to set off an idea within a sentence. Dashes, however, call attention to the set-off idea in a way that parentheses do not:

> Taipei 101 (then the tallest building in the world) was completed in 2005.

> Taipei 101—then the tallest building in the world—was completed in 2005.

A dash may also be used in place of a colon to set off a word or phrase at the end of a sentence:

> He fainted when he heard how much he had won: one million dollars.

> He fainted when he heard how much he had won—one million dollars.

When typing, you may use two hyphens (with no space before or after them) to form a dash.

24. PARENTHESES

Parentheses are used to set off an interruption in the middle of a sentence, or to make a point which is not part of the main flow of the sentence. They are frequently used to give examples, or to express something in other words. Example:

> Several world leaders of the 1980s (Deng in China, Reagan in the US, etc.) were very old men.

25. SQUARE BRACKETS

Square brackets are used for parentheses within parentheses, or to show that the words within the parentheses are added to a quotation by another person.

> Lentricchia claims that "in reading James' Preface [to *What Maisie Knew*] one is struck as much by what is omitted as by what is revealed."

26. THE APOSTROPHE

The two main uses of the apostrophe are to show possession (e.g., "Peter's book") and to shorten certain common word combinations (e.g., *can't, shouldn't, he's*).

26a. CONTRACTIONS

Contractions should be avoided in formal written work. Use *cannot*, not *can't*; *did not*, not *didn't*; and so on.

informal	The experiment wasn't a success, because we'd heated the solution to too high a temperature.
more formal	The experiment was not a success, because we had heated the solution to too high a temperature.

26b. POSSESSION
(See also **its/it's**, page 205.)

The correct placing of the apostrophe to show possession can be a tricky matter. When the noun is singular, the apostrophe must come before the *s* (e.g., *Peter's, George's, Canada's*), whereas when the noun is plural and ends in an *s* already, the apostrophe comes after the *s*.

worth checking	His parent's house is filled with antiques.
revised	His parents' house is filled with antiques.

Note that no apostrophe is needed when a plural is not possessive.

needs checking	His parent's were away for the weekend.
revised	His parents were away for the weekend.

When a singular noun already ends in *s*, authorities differ as to whether or not a second *s* should be added after the apostrophe:

correct	Ray Charles' music has been very influential.
correct	Ray Charles's music has been very influential.

Whichever convention a writer chooses, he should be consistent. And be sure in such cases not to put the apostrophe before the first *s*.

needs checking	Shield's novel is finely, yet delicately constructed. (concerning novelist Carol Shields)
revised	Shields' novel is finely, yet delicately constructed. (or "Shields's novel")

27. QUOTATION MARKS

The main use of quotation marks is to show that the exact words spoken or written are being repeated. The main rules for writing direct speech in English are as follows:

- The exact words spoken—and no other words—must be surrounded by quotation marks.
- According to North American convention, closing punctuation should be placed inside the quotation marks.

- With each change in speaker a new paragraph should be begun.

needs checking	He shouted, "The house is on fire"!
revised	He shouted, "The house is on fire!"

Note that passages of direct speech should not be presented as if they were indirect speech.

needs checking	The official indicated that, "We are not prepared to allow galloping inflation."
revised	The official said, "We are not prepared to allow galloping inflation."
or	The official indicated that his government was not prepared to allow galloping inflation.

In a formal essay, any quotation longer than four lines should normally be indented to set it off from the body of the text. Any quotation of more than three lines from a poem should also be set off and indented. Quotations set off from the body of the text in this way should not be preceded or followed by quotation marks.

27a. OTHER USES OF QUOTATION MARKS

According to different conventions, words that are being mentioned rather than used may be set off by quotation marks, single quotation marks, or italics:

The words "except" and "accept" are sometimes confused.

The words 'except' and 'accept' are sometimes confused.

The words *except* and *accept* are sometimes confused.

Quotation marks (or single quotation marks) are sometimes also used to indicate that the writer does not endorse the quoted statement, claim, or description.

Quotation marks are usually used in this way only with a word or brief phrase. When so used they have the connotation of *supposed* or *so-called*; they suggest that the quoted word or phrase is either euphemistic or downright false:

> After a workout the weightlifters would each consume a "snack" of a steak sandwich, half a dozen eggs, several pieces of bread and butter, and a quart of tomato juice.

In the following two versions of the same report the more sparing use of quotation marks in the second version signals clearly to the reader the writer's scepticism as to the honesty of the quoted claim.

> President Charez appeared to stagger as he left the plane. "The President is feeling tired and emotional," his Press Secretary later reported.

> A "tired and emotional" President Charez appeared to stagger as he left the plane.

27b. MISUSE OF QUOTATION MARKS TO INDICATE EMPHASIS

Quotation marks (unlike italics, bold letters, capital letters, or underlining) should never be used to try to lend emphasis to a particular word or phrase. Because quotation marks may be used to convey the sense *supposed* or *so-called* (see above), the common misuse of quotation marks to try to lend emphasis often creates ludicrous effects.

needs checking	All our bagels are served "fresh" daily.
	(The unintended suggestion here is that the claim of freshness is a dubious one.)
revised	All our bagels are served fresh daily.
or	All our bagels are served **fresh** daily.
	(if emphasis is required in an advertisement)

27c. SINGLE QUOTATION MARKS

In North America the main use of single quotation marks is to mark quotations within quotations:

> According to the Press Secretary, "When the Minister said, 'I never inhaled,' he meant it."

Depending on convention, single quotation marks may also be used to show that a word or phrase is being mentioned rather than used (see above).

In the United Kingdom and some other countries, quotation marks and single quotation marks are used for direct speech in precisely the opposite way that North Americans use them; single quotation marks (or inverted commas, as they are sometimes called) are used for direct speech, and double marks are used for quotations within quotations. Here is the correct British version of the above sentence:

> According to the Press Secretary, 'When the Minister said, "I never inhaled", he meant it'.

Note here that the UK usage also places the closing punctuation marks outside the closing quotation marks.

28. ELLIPSES

Three dots are used to indicate the omission of one or more words needed to complete a sentence or other grammatical construction. Note that when used in a quotation an ellipsis comes *inside* the quotation marks, and that when an ellipsis precedes the end of a sentence, there should be a total of *four* dots.

ON THE WEB

Exercises on punctuation may be found at
www.broadviewpress.com/writing.
Click on **Exercises** and go to **F1–F21**.

FORMAT AND SPELLING

29. CAPITALIZATION

Proper nouns (naming specific persons, places, or things) should always be capitalized. Common nouns are not normally capitalized. Here are a few examples:

PROPER	COMMON
June	summer
Parliament of Canada	in parliament
Mother (used as a name)	my mother
Remembrance Day	in remembrance
Memorial Day	as a memorial
National Gallery	a gallery
Director	a director
Professor	a professor
the Enlightenment	the eighteenth century
the Restoration (historical period in England)	the restoration (other uses of the word)
the Renaissance	a renaissance
God	a god
Catholic (belonging to that particular church)	catholic (meaning *wide-ranging* or *universal*)
a Liberal (belonging to the Liberal Party)	a liberal (holding liberal ideas)
a Democrat (belonging to the Democratic Party)	a democrat (believing in democratic ideals)

Names of academic subjects are not capitalized (unless they are names of languages).

Major words in the titles of books, articles, stories, poems, films, and so on should be capitalized; articles, short prepositions, and conjunctions are not normally capitalized unless they are the first word of a title or subtitle.

needs checking	She became a Director of the company in 2009.
revised	She became a director of the company in 2009.
or	She became a member of the Board of Directors in 2009.

needs checking	Robert Boardman discusses *The Bridge On The River Kwai* extensively in his book.
revised	Robert Boardman discusses *The Bridge on the River Kwai* extensively in his book.

30. ABBREVIATIONS

Abbreviations are a convenient way of presenting information in a smaller amount of space. This section discusses conventions for using abbreviations in formal writing.

30a. TITLES

Titles are normally abbreviated when used immediately before or after a person's full name.

Mr. Isaiah Thomas
Sammy Davis Jr.
Dr. Jane Phelps
Marcia Gibbs, MD

When using a title together with the last name only, the full title should be written out.

Prof. Marc Ereshefsky   Professor Ereshefsky
Sen. Keith Davey   Senator Davey

30b. ACADEMIC AND BUSINESS TERMS

Common abbreviations are acceptable in formal writing so long as they are likely to be readily understood. Otherwise, the full name should be written out when first used and the abbreviation given in parentheses. Thereafter, the abbreviation may be used on its own.

The Atomic Energy Commission (AEC) has broad-ranging regulatory authority.

The American Philosophical Association (APA) holds three large regional meetings annually.

30c. LATIN ABBREVIATIONS

Several abbreviations of Latin terms are common in formal academic writing:

cf.	compare (Latin *confer*)
e.g.	for example (Latin *exempli gratia*)
et al.	and others (Latin *et alia*)
etc.	and so on (Latin *et cetera*)
i.e.	that is (Latin *id est*)
NB	note well (Latin *nota bene*)

31. NUMBERS

Numbers of one or two words should be written out. Use figures for all other numbers.

needs checking   The building is 72 storeys tall.
revised   The building is seventy-two storeys tall.

The same principle applies for dollar figures (or figures in other currencies).

needs checking   She lent her brother 10 dollars.
revised   She lent her brother ten dollars.

It is acceptable to combine figures and words for very large numbers:

The government is projecting a $200 billion deficit.

In general, figures should be used in addresses, dates, percentages, and reports of scores or statistics.

needs checking   In the third game of the tournament, Canada and the Czech Republic tied three three.
revised   In the third game of the tournament, Canada and the Czech Republic tied 3–3.

32. ITALICS

Italics may be represented in handwritten or typed papers by underlining. Italics serve several different functions. While the titles of short stories, poems, and other short works are set off by quotation marks, titles of longer works and the names of newspapers, magazines, and so on should appear in italics:

"The Dead"	*Dubliners*
"Burnt Norton"	*Four Quartets*
"Budget Controversy Continues"	*The Economist*
"Smells like Teen Spirit"	*Nevermind*

Italics are also used for the names of paintings and sculptures, television series, and software.

Italics are also used for words or phrases from other languages in written English.

needs checking	The play ends with an appearance of a deus ex machina.
revised	The play ends with an appearance of a *deus ex machina.*

Either italics or quotation marks may be used to indicate that words are mentioned rather than used. (See above, under **quotation marks**.)

Finally, italics are often used to provide special emphasis that is not otherwise clear from the context or the structure of the sentence.

33. SPELLING

The wittiest example of the illogic of English spelling remains Bernard Shaw's famous spelling of *fish* as *ghoti*. The *gh* sounds like the *gh* in *enough*; the *o* sounds like the *o* in *women* (once spelled *wimmen*, incidentally); and the *ti* sounds like the *ti* in *nation* or *station*. Shaw passionately advocated a rationalization of English spelling; it still has not happened, and probably never will.

Perhaps the best way to learn correct spelling is to be tested by someone else, or to test yourself every week on a different group of words. For example, you might learn the words from the list below beginning with a and b one week, the words beginning with c and d the next week, and so on.

33a. SPELL-CHECK

No computer can be a substitute for careful proofreading. Spell-check is wonderful, but it cannot tell if it is your friend or your fiend, or if you have signed off a letter with best wishes or beast wishes.

33b. SPELLING AND SOUND

Many spelling mistakes result from similarities in the pronunciation of words with very different meanings. These are covered in the list below. Other words that cause spelling difficulties are listed separately.

absent (adjective)	absence (noun)
absorb	absorption
accept	except
access (entry)	excess (too much)
advice (noun)	advise (verb)
affect (to influence)	effect (result)
allowed (permitted)	aloud
alter (change)	altar (in a church)
appraise (value)	apprise (inform)
base (foundation)	bass (in music)
bath (noun)	bathe (verb)
berry (fruit)	bury (the dead)
beside (by the side of)	besides (as well as)
birth	berth (bed)
bitten	beaten
bizarre (strange)	bazaar (market)
bloc (political grouping)	block
breath (noun)	breathe (verb)
buoy (in the water)	boy
buy (purchase)	by

cash	cache (hiding place)
casual (informal)	causal (to do with causes)
cause	case
ceased (stopped)	seized (grabbed)
ceiling (above you)	sealing
chick	cheek
chose (past tense)	choose (present tense)
cite (make reference to)	sight/site
climatic	climactic
cloths (fabric)	clothes
coma (unconscious)	comma (punctuation)
compliment (praise)	complement (make complete)
conscious (aware)	conscience (sense of right)
contract	construct
conventional (usual)	convectional
conversation	conservation/concentration
convinced	convicted (of a crime)
cord (rope)	chord (music)
council (group)	counsel (advice)
course	coarse (rough)
credible (believable)	creditable (deserving credit)
critic (one who criticizes)	critique (piece of criticism)
defer (show respect)	differ
deference (respect)	difference
deprecate (criticize)	depreciate (reduce in value)
desert (dry place)	dessert (sweet)
device (thing)	devise (to plan)
died/had died	dead/was dead
dissent (protest)	descent (downward motion)
distant (adjective)	distance (noun)
edition (of a book etc.)	addition (something added)
emigrant	immigrant
envelop (verb)	envelope (noun)
except	expect
fear	fair/fare (payment)
feeling	filling
fell	feel/fill
flaunt (display)	flout
formally	formerly (previously)
forth (forward)	fourth (after third)
forward	foreword (in a book)
foul	fowl (birds)
future	feature

genus (biological type)	genius (creative intelligence)
greet	great/grate (scrape)
guerillas (fighters)	gorillas (apes)
guided (led)	guarded (protected)
had	heard/head
heat	heart/hate
heir (inheritor)	air
human	humane (kind)
illicit (not permitted)	elicit (bring forth)
illusion (unreal image)	allusion (reference)
immigrate	emigrate
independent (adjective)	independence (noun)
inhabit (live in)	inhibit (retard)
instance (occurrence)	instants (moments)
intense (concentrating)	intents
isle (island)	aisle (to walk in)
kernel	colonel
know	no/now
lack	lake
later	latter/letter
lath (piece of wood)	lathe (machine)
lead	led
leave	leaf
leave	live
leaving	living
lessen (reduce)	lesson
let	late
lightning (from clouds)	lightening (becoming lighter)
lose (be unable to find)	loose (not tight)
mad (insane)	maid (servant)
man	men
martial (to do with fighting)	marshal
mental	metal
merry	marry
met	meet/mate
minor (underage)	miner (underground)
mist (light fog)	missed
moral (ethical)	morale (spirit)
mourning (after death)	morning
new	knew
of	off
on	own
ones	once

pain — pane (of glass)
patients (sick people) — patience (ability to wait)
peer (look closely) — pier (wharf)
perpetrate (be guilty of) — perpetuate (cause to continue)
perquisite (privilege) — prerequisite (requirement)
personal (private) — personnel (employees)
perspective (vision) — prospective (anticipated)
poor — pour (liquid)/pore
precede (go before) — proceed (continue)
precedent — president
price (cost) — prize (reward)
prostate — prostrate
quay (wharf—pronounced key) — key

quite — quiet (not noisy)
rein (to control animals) — rain/reign
release (let go) — realize (discover)
relieve (verb) — relief (noun)
response (noun) — responds (verb)
rid — ride
ridden — written
rise — rice
rite (ritual) — right/write
rod — rode/reared
rote (repetition) — wrote
saved — served
saw — seen
saw — so/sew
scene (location) — seen
seam (in clothes etc.) — seem (appear)
secret — sacred (holy)
sell (verb) — sail (boat)
senses — census (population count)
shed — shade
shone — shown
shot — short
sit — sat/set
smell — smile
snake — snack (small meal)
soar — sore (hurt)
sole (single) — soul (spirit)
sort (type or kind) — sought (looked for)
steal (present tense) — stole (past tense)

straight (not crooked)	strait (of water)
striped (e.g. a zebra)	stripped (uncovered)
suite (rooms or music)	suit/sweet
super	supper (meal)
suppose	supposed to
sympathies (noun)	sympathize (verb)
tale (story)	tail
talk	took
tap	tape
than	then
they	there/their
thing	think
this	these
throw	threw (past tense)
tied	tired
urban (in cities)	urbane (sophisticated)
vanish (disappear)	varnish
vein (to carry blood)	vain
waist (your middle)	waste
wait	weight (heaviness)
waive (give up)	wave
wants	once
weak (not strong)	week
weather (sunny, wet, etc.)	whether (or not)
wedding	weeding
were	where
wholly (completely)	holy (sacred)/holly
woman	women
won	worn
yoke (for animals)	yolk (of an egg)

33c. AMERICAN SPELLING, BRITISH SPELLING, CANADIAN SPELLING

A number of words that cause spelling difficulties are spelled differently in different countries. In the following list the British spelling is on the right, the American on the left. Either is correct in Canada, so long as the writer is consistent.

behavior	behaviour
center	centre

cigaret	cigarette
color	colour
defense	defence
favor	favour
favorite	favourite
fulfill	fulfil
humor	humour
likable	likeable
maneuver	manoeuvre
marvelous	marvellous
neighbor	neighbour
omelet	omelette
program	programme
Shakespearian	Shakespearean
skeptical	sceptical
skillful	skilful
theater	theatre
traveling	travelling

33d. OTHER SPELLING MISTAKES

Following is a list of some other commonly
misspelled words.

abbreviation	ammonia	approach
absence	amoeba	architect
accelerator	among	arguable
accident	amortize	argument
accidentally	amount	arsonist
accommodation	anachronism	arteriosclerosis
achieve	analogous	artillery
acknowledge	analysis	asinine
acquire	anchor	author
acquisition	androgynous	auxiliary
acquit	annihilate	bacteria
acre	antecedent	basically
across	anti-Semitic	battery
address	anxious	beautiful
adjacent	apocalypse	beginning
advertisement	apparatus	believe
affidavit	apparently	boast
ambulance	appreciate	boastful

breakfast
bulletin
burglar
burial
buried
business
candidate
capillary
cappuccino
Caribbean
carpentry
cautious
ceiling
changeable
character
chlorophyll
choir
cholesterol
chrome
chromosome
chronological
chrysalis
chrysanthemum
coincidence
colleague
colonel
colossal
column
commitment
committee
comparative
competition
competitor
complexion
conceive
condemn
conjunction
connoisseur
consensus
consistent
controller
convenience
cooperation

cooperative
courteous
courtesy
creator
creature
criticism
cyst
decisive
definite
delicious
description
desirable
despair
despise
destroy
develop
diesel
different
dilemma
dining
disappear
disappoint
disastrous
discrimination
disease
disintegrate
dissatisfied
dominate
dormitory
double
doubtful
drunkard
drunkenness
duchess
due
dying
eclipse
effective
efficient
eighth
embarrass
employee
encourage

enemy
enmity
enormous
entertain
enthusiasm
entitle
entrepreneur
environment
enzyme
epidermis
epididymis
erroneous
esophagus
especially
espresso
essential
exaggerate
excessive
excite
exercise
exhilaration
existence
existent
experience
extraordinary
Fahrenheit
faithful
faithfully
farinaceous
fault
financial
foreigner
foretell
forty
fourth
gauge
gamete
germination
government
grammar
grateful
gruesome
guarantee

guerrillas
guilty
happened
happiest
hatred
hectare
helpful
hyena
hypothesis
ichthyology
idiosyncratic
imaginary
imagine
immersible
immigration
impeccable
importance
impresario
inchoate
incomprehensible
independent
indestructible
indigenous
indispensable
ineffable
infinitesimal
inoculate
insufferable
intention
intentional
interrupt
irrelevant
irresponsible
isosceles
isthmus
itinerary
jealous
jeopardy
journalist
jump
junction
kneel
knowledge

knowledgeable
laboratories
laboratory
language
lazy, laziness
ledger
leisure
liaise, liaison
liberation
library
licence
lieutenant
liquid, liquefy
literature
lying
medicine
medieval
membrane
merciful
mermaid
millennia
millennium
millionaire
minuscule
mischief
mischievous
naked
naughty
necessary
necessity
noticeable
nuclear
nucleus
obscene
obsolescent
obsolete
occasion
occasional
occupy
occur
occurred
occurrence
omit

ourselves
paid
parallel
parliament
parliamentary
party
permissible
permission
perpendicular
perseverance
photosynthesis
playful
possess
possession
poultry
predictable
pregnancy
pregnant
prerogative
prescription
privilege
properly
psychiatric
psychological
punctuation
pursue
questionnaire
really
receipt
recommend
referee
reference
regret
repeat
repetition
replies
reply
residence (place)
residents (people)
restaurant
revolutionary
rheumatism
rhododendron

rhombus
rhubarb
rhyme
rhythm
saddest
sandals
scene
schedule
schizophrenic
science
scintillate
scissors
scream
scrumptious
search
seize
sense
separate
shining
shotgun
sigh
significant
simultaneous
sincerely
slippery
slogan
smart
solemn

spaghetti
speech
spongy
sponsor
stale
stingy
stomach
stubborn
studious
studying
stupefy
stupid
subordinate
subpoena
substitute
subtle, subtlety
suburbs
succeed
success, successful
sue, suing
summary
surprised
surreptitious
surrounded
survive
symbol
talkative
tarred

television
temperature
tendency
theoretical
theory
title
tough
tragedy
trophy
truly
unique
until
vacancy
vacillate
valuable
vegetable
vehicle
vicious
visitor
volume
voluntary
Wednesday
welcome
whisper
writer
writing
written
yield

ON THE WEB

Exercises on spelling and on capitalization
may be found at

www.broadviewpress.com/writing.

Click on **Exercises** and go to **F28–F38**.

DOCUMENTATION

34. CITATION AND DOCUMENTATION

There are two chief concerns when it comes to citing and documenting material: accuracy and consistency. Whatever system of citation is used, a research writer must follow it closely and consistently. Four of the most commonly used systems of citation are summarized in these pages: MLA style, APA style, Chicago style, and CSE style. It may also be helpful to consult exemplary essays. (A selection of these may be found on the website associated with this book:
www.broadviewpress.com/writing.)

34a. CITATION AND PLAGIARISM

To take the words or ideas of another without properly acknowledging them is to commit plagiarism—a serious form of dishonesty. Plagiarism is subject to serious penalties at all academic institutions; these may range from a failing grade being assigned for the relevant course to outright expulsion from the institution.

The avoidance of plagiarism begins with careful research so as to remove any chance of your confusing someone else's words for your own during the writing process. Judgement of the crime of plagiarism, incidentally, makes no provision for malice aforethought; whether or not a writer is wilfully deceptive makes no difference. Therefore, competent writers keep thorough and well-organized notes while reading and researching—notes that clearly indicate where each idea comes from and when the exact words used by another writer are being jotted down.

If you summarize or paraphrase someone else's work without using the exact words that they use, you do not need to use quotation marks—but you must still cite the work.

> Researchers have shown that the model of genetic mapping first advanced by Crick and Watson leaves many questions unanswered (Commoner 42).

Do you need a citation for everything? No. Obviously citations are not needed when you are putting forward your own original ideas. Nor are they necessary when you are touching on common knowledge. If you refer to the population of China or the date when the North American Free Trade Agreement was signed, you do not need to provide any citation, since such information is generally available and widely known.

34b. SIGNAL PHRASES

If you quote the exact words of a source, rather than summarize or paraphrase, it is important to integrate the quotation into the body of your writing. You must not drop quoted phrases or sentences in amongst your own; instead, you must signal to the reader where the quoted material comes from and how it connects to your own argument. To this end, phrases such as the following are very useful:

> As Smith and Jones have demonstrated, "...
> In the words of one researcher, "...
> In his most recent book McGann advances the view that, as he puts it, "...
> As Nussbaum observes, "...
> Kendal suggests that "...
> Murphy and other scholars have rejected these claims, arguing that "...
> Morgan has emphasized this point in her recent research: "...
> As Sayeed puts it, "...
> To be sure, Mtele allows that "...
> In his later novels Hardy takes a bleaker view, frequently suggesting that "...

Phrases such as those above are known as signal phrases: they signal to the reader that the research of another is being referred to. Here is a fuller list of words and expressions that may be useful in signal phrases:

according to _____, "...	finds
acknowledges	grants
adds	illustrates
admits	implies
advances	in the view of _____,
agrees	"...
allows	in the words of
argues	_____, "...
asserts	insists
attests	intimates
believes	notes
claims	observes
comments	points out
compares	puts it
concludes	reasons
confirms	refutes
contends	rejects
declares	reports
demonstrates	responds
denies	suggests
disputes	takes issue with
emphasizes	thinks
endorses	writes

needs checking   Many critics and theorists of the past
generation have been in no doubt as to
the perniciousness of Conrad's
attitudes. "Conrad was a bloody racist"
(Achebe 788). But others have taken a
more nuanced view.

(Here the Achebe quotation has been dropped
into the text.)

revised   Many critics and theorists of the past
generation have been in no doubt as to

the perniciousness of Conrad's attitudes. Achebe's influential 1977 article is perhaps the most unequivocal statement of this view: "Conrad was a bloody racist" (788), Achebe asserts. But others have taken a more nuanced view.

(Here the same quotation has been integrated into the surrounding text.)

In academic writing prose quotations of more than four lines and verse quotations of more than three lines should be indented, without surrounding quotations marks. Longer quotations also need signals; they need to be introduced in a way that integrates them into the text of your essay. Normally this is done with a sentence ending with a colon.

Edward Said sets Conrad's fiction in the context of its original readers:

> Conrad's readers of the time were not expected to ask about or concern themselves with what became of the natives. What mattered to them was how Marlow makes sense of everything.... This is a short step away from King Leopold's account of his International Congo Association "rendering lasting and disinterested services" to the cause of progress. (200)

Yet Conrad himself unequivocally described the activities Leopold sponsored as "the vilest scramble for loot that ever disfigured the history of human conscience" ("Geography" 17).

The lines of long verse quotations should be arranged just as they are in the original.

The ending of Margaret Avison's "September Street" moves from the decaying, discordant city toward a glimpse of an outer/inner infinitude:

> On the yellow porch
>   one sits, not reading headlines; the old eyes
> read far out into the mild
>   air, runes.
>
> See. There: a stray sea-gull. (lines 20-24)

In short verse quotations, lines should be separated from one another by a forward slash with a space on either side of it.

Pope's "Epistle II. To a Lady," in its vivid portrayal of wasted lives, sharply criticizes the social values that render older women superfluous objects of contempt: "Still round and round the Ghosts of Beauty glide, / And haunt the places where their Honour dy'd" (lines 241-42).

35. MLA STYLE

A sample of an essay using MLA style appears at the end of this section (page 118). Additional sample essays using MLA style appear on the Broadview website. Key points about parenthetical referencing and "Works Cited" lists presented according to the MLA style guidelines appear below. *The MLA Handbook for Writers of Research Papers* (7th edition 2009) should be consulted for more detailed questions—or they may be answerable at the website of the MLA, www.mla.org, where updates and answers to frequently asked questions are posted.

SUMMARY LIST: Parenthetical Referencing

1. parenthetical referencing
2. titles: italics/quotation marks
3. placing of parenthetical references
4. parenthetical reference when text is in parentheses
5. no signal phrase (or author not named in signal phrase)
6. page number unavailable
7. one page or less
8. page, section, or paragraph numbers all unavailable
9. multiple authors
10. author unknown/corporate author
11. electronic source—author not given
12. more than one work by the same author cited
13. multi-volume works
14. two or more authors with the same last name
15. indirect quotations
16. short poems
17. longer poems
18. novels or short stories
19. plays
20. literary texts cited from the Web
21. sacred texts
22. works in an anthology or book of readings

SUMMARY LIST: Works Cited

1. single author
2. two or three authors
3. four or more authors

4. corporate author

5. works with no author

6. two or more works by the same author

7. edited works

8. works in translation

9. selections from anthologies or collections of readings

10. multi-volume works

11. different editions

12. reference work entries

13. works with a title in the title

14. material from prefaces, introductions, etc.

15. films, programs, interviews, performances, music, art

16. magazine articles

17. newspaper articles

18. journal articles

19. book reviews

20. periodical publications in online databases

21. online projects

22. online books

23. information databases

24. publication on a CD-ROM or DVD-ROM

25. posting to a discussion list

26. electronic sources—other information

35a. ABOUT PARENTHETICAL REFERENCING

1. parenthetical referencing: Under the MLA system a quotation or specific reference to another work is followed by a parenthetical page reference:

Bonnycastle refers to "the true and lively spirit of opposition" with which Marxist literary criticism invigorates the discipline (204).

The work is then listed under "Works Cited" at the end of the essay:

Bonnycastle, Stephen. *In Search of Authority: An Introductory Guide to Literary Theory.* 3rd ed. Peterborough: Broadview, 2007. Print.

(See below for information about the "Works Cited" list.)

2. titles: italics/quotation marks: Notice in the above example that both the title and the subtitle are in italics. Italicize the titles of works that are not part of other works (that is, that are published or offered as "stand alone" works). Examples include titles of books (*Oryx and Crake*), magazines (*The New Yorker*), newspapers (*The Guardian*), journals (*The American Poetry Review*), websites (*The Camelot Project*), films (*Memento*), television shows (*The X-Files*), and compact discs, audiocassettes, or record albums (*Dark Side of the Moon*).

Don't italicize but do put into double quotation marks the titles of works that are part of other, longer works. Examples include chapters in books ("The Autist Artist" in *The Man Who Mistook His Wife for a Hat and Other Clinical Tales*), encyclopedia articles ("Existentialism"), essays in books ("Salvation in the Garden: Daoism and Ecology" in *Daoism and Ecology: Ways within a Cosmic Landscape*), short stories ("Young Goodman Brown"), poems ("Daddy"), pages on websites ("The Fisher King" from *The Camelot Project*), episodes of television shows ("Small Potatoes" from *The X-Files*), and songs ("Eclipse" from *Dark Side of the Moon*). Put the titles of public lectures in double quotation marks as well ("Walls in the *Epic of Gilgamesh*").

Notice that the last example features a book title within a lecture title, and that the book title is in italics, according to the convention outlined above. If the title of a stand-alone work contains the title of a work that is not independent, the latter is put in double quotation marks, and the entire title is put in italics (*"Self-Reliance" and Other Essays*). If the title of a stand-alone work appears within the title of another independent work, MLA recommends that the former be put in italics and the latter not (*Chaucer's* House of Fame: *The Poetics of Skeptical Fideism*). If the title of a non-independent work is embedded in another title of the same kind, put the inner title into single quotation marks and the outer title in double quotation marks ("The Drama of Donne's 'The Indifferent'").

3. placing of parenthetical references: Place parenthetical references at the ends of clauses or sentences in order to keep disruption of your writing to a minimum. The parenthetical reference comes before the period or comma in the surrounding sentence. (If the quotation ends with punctuation other than a period or comma, then this should precede the end of the quotation, and a period or comma should still follow the parenthetical reference.)

> Ricks refuted this point early on (16), but the claim has continued to be made in recent years.

> In "The Windhover," on the other hand, Hopkins bubbles over; "the mastery of the thing!" (8), he enthuses when he thinks of a bird, and he exclaims shortly thereafter, "O my chevalier!" (10).

When a cited quotation is set off from the text, however, the parenthetical reference should be placed after the concluding punctuation.

> Muriel Jaeger draws on the following anecdote in discussing the resistance of many wealthy Victorians to the idea of widespread education for the poor:

>> In a mischievous mood, Henry Brougham once told [some well-off acquaintances who were] showing perturbation about the likely results of educating the "lower orders" that they could maintain their superiority by working harder themselves. (105)

4. parenthetical reference when text is in parentheses: If a parenthetical reference occurs within text in parentheses, square brackets are used for the reference.

> The development of a mass literary culture (or a "print culture," to use Williams's expression [88]) took several hundred years in Britain.

5. no signal phrase (or author not named in signal phrase): If the context does not make it clear who the author is, that information must be added to the parenthetical reference. Note that no comma separates the name of the author from the page number.

> Even in recent years some have continued to believe that Marxist literary criticism invigorates the discipline with a "true and lively spirit of opposition" (Bonnycastle 204).

6. page number unavailable: Many Internet sources lack page numbers. In that case you should not rely on the page number of a printout on your printer, as page breaks may differ with different printers. Instead, provide a section or paragraph number if possible.

> Bhabha clearly implies that he finds such an approach objectionable (par. 7).

> In a recent Web posting a leading critic has clearly implied that he finds such an approach objectionable (Bhabha, par. 7).

> In "The American Scholar" Emerson asserts that America's "long apprenticeship to the learning of other lands" is drawing to a close (par. 1).

Notice that (unlike with page numbers) MLA style requires a comma between author and paragraph number in a citation.

7. one page or less: If a source is one page long or less, it is advisable to still provide the page number (though MLA does not require this).

> In an article in the online edition of *The Chicago Tribune*, Bosley says that he finds the writing of the novel "excruciating" (1).

8. page, section, or paragraph numbers all unavailable: In some cases a source may be more than one page long but neither section nor paragraph numbers may be available. If so, it may be best to lead into the quotation without using a signal phrase; the citation in that case will provide only the author's name.

> In a manifesto issued in 2001, the artist advances a radically different approach (Mbeki).

9. multiple authors: If there are two or three authors, all authors should be named either in the signal phrase or in the parenthetical reference.

> Chambliss and Best argue that the importance of this novel is primarily historical (233).

> Two distinguished scholars have recently argued that the importance of this novel is primarily historical (Chambliss and Best 233).

four authors/more authors: In the parenthetical reference, you have two options, but whichever you choose should match the format of the corresponding entry in Works Cited. You may use only the first author's name, followed by *et al.*, short for the Latin *et alia*, meaning *and others* (Fromkin et al. 34–36), or you may list the last names of all the authors in the order in which they appear in the original work (Fromkin, Rodman, Hultin, and Logan 34–36).

10. author unknown/corporate author: Be
sure to refer to the relevant organization and/or the title
of the piece so as to make the reference clear. Shorten a
long title to avoid awkwardness, but be sure that the
shortened version begins with the same word as the corresponding entry in "Works Cited" so that readers can
move easily from the citation to the bibliographic information. For example, *Comparative Indo-European
Linguistics: An Introduction* should be shortened to
Comparative Indo-European rather than *Indo-European
Linguistics*. The first two examples below cite unsigned
newspaper or encyclopedia articles; the last is a corporate author parenthetical citation.

> As *The New York Times* reported in one of its several
> December 2 articles on the Florida recount, Vice-
> President Gore looked tired and strained as he
> answered questions ("Gore Press Conference" A16).

> According to the *Columbia Encyclopedia*, in the
> 1990s Sao Paulo began to rapidly overtake Mexico
> City as the world's most polluted city ("Air Pollution"
> 21).

> There are a number of organizations mandated "to
> foster the production and enjoyment of the arts in
> Canada" (Canada Council for the Arts 2).

11. electronic source—author not given: If
the author of the electronic source is not given, it may be
identified in the parenthetical reference by a short form
of the title (see the advice on shortening titles in section
10 above).

> During the campaign the party's electronic newsletter
> mentioned the candidate's leading role in the recent
> protests ("Globalization," par. 4).

12. more than one work by the same author cited: If you include more than one work by the same author in your list of works cited, you must make clear which work is being cited each time. This may be done either by mentioning the work in a signal phrase or by including in the citation a short version of the title.

> In *The House of Mirth*, for example, Wharton writes of love as keeping Lily and Selden "from atrophy and extinction" (282).

> Wharton sees love as possessing the power to keep humans "from atrophy and extinction" (*House of Mirth* 282).

13. multi-volume works: Note, by number, the volume you are referring to, followed by a colon, before noting the page number. Use the abbreviation "vol." when citing an entire volume.

> Towards the end of *In Darkest Africa* Stanley refers to the Victoria Falls (2:387).

> Metatextuality is a dominant feature in the later scenes of the graphic novel *Maus* (Spiegelman, vol. 2).

14. two or more authors with the same last name: If the Works Cited list includes two or more authors with the same last name, the parenthetical reference should supply both first initials and last names, or, if the first initials are also the same, the full first and last names:

> One of the leading economists of the time advocated wage and price controls (Harry Johnston 197).

15. indirect quotations: When an original source is not available but is referred to by another source, the parenthetical reference includes *qtd. in* (an abbreviation of *quoted in*) and a reference to the second source. In the example below, Casewell is quoted by Bouvier; the parenthetical reference directs readers to an entry in Works Cited for the Bouvier work.

> Casewell considers Lambert's position to be "outrageously arrogant" (qtd. in Bouvier 59).

Literary Works

The underlying principle of the parenthetical reference system is the same regardless of the type of work one is citing—to make it as easy as possible for your reader to find the reference.

16. short poems: For short poems, cite line numbers rather than page numbers.

> In "Dover Beach" Arnold hears the pebbles in the waves bring the "eternal note of sadness in" (line 14).

If you are citing the same poem repeatedly, use just the numbers for subsequent references.

> The world, in Arnold's view, has "really neither joy, nor love, nor light" (33).

17. longer poems: For longer poems with parts, cite the part (or section, or "book") as well as the line (where available). Use Arabic numerals, and use a period for separation.

> In "Ode: Intimations of Immortality" Wordsworth calls human birth "but a sleep and a forgetting" (5.1).

18. novels or short stories: When a work of prose fiction has chapters or numbered divisions the citation should include first the page number, and then book, chapter, and section numbers as applicable. (These can be very useful in helping readers of a different edition to locate the passage you are citing.) Arabic numerals should be used. A semicolon should be used to separate the page number from the other information.

> When Joseph and Fanny are by themselves, they immediately express their affection for each other, or, as Fielding puts it, "solace themselves" with "amorous discourse" (151; ch. 26).

> In *Tender Is the Night* Dick's ambition does not quite crowd out the desire for love: "He wanted to be loved too, if he could fit it in" (133; bk. 2, ch. 4).

19. plays: Almost all plays are divided into acts and/or scenes. For plays that do not include line numbering throughout, cite the page number in the edition you have been using, followed by act and/or scene numbers as applicable:

> As Angie and Joyce begin drinking together Angie pronounces the occasion "better than Christmas" (72; act 3).

> Near the conclusion of Inchbald's *Wives as They Were* Bronzely declares that he has been "made to think with reverence on the matrimonial compact" (62; act 5, sc. 4).

For plays written entirely or largely in verse, where line numbers are typically provided throughout, you should omit the reference to page number in the citation. Instead, cite the act, scene, and line numbers, using Arabic numerals. For a Shakespeare play, if the title isn't clear from the introduction to a quotation, an abbreviation of the title may also be used. The parenthetical reference below is for Shakespeare's *The Merchant of Venice*, Act 2, Scene 3, lines 2–4:

> Jessica clearly has some fondness for Launcelot: "Our house is hell, and thou, a merry devil, / Dost rob it of some taste of tediousness. / But fare thee well; there is a ducat for thee" (*MV* 2.3 2–4).

20. literary texts cited from the Web: If you are citing literary texts where you have consulted editions on the Web, the principles are exactly the same, except that you need not cite page numbers. For example, if the online Gutenberg edition of Fielding's *Joseph Andrews* were being cited, the citation would be as follows:

> When Joseph and Fanny are by themselves, they immediately express their affection for each other, or, as Fielding puts it, "solace themselves" with "amorous discourse" (ch. 26).

Students should be cautioned that online editions of literary texts are often unreliable. Typically there are far more typos and other errors in online versions of literary texts than there are in print versions, and such things as the layout of poems are also often unreliable. It is often possible to exercise judgement about such matters, however. If, for example, you are not required to base your essay on a particular copy of a Thomas Hardy poem but may find your own, you will be far better off using the text you will find on the Representative Poetry Online site run out of the University of Toronto than you will using a text you might find on a "World's Finest Love Poems" site.

21. sacred texts: The Bible and other sacred texts

that are available in many editions should be cited in a way that enables the reader to check the reference in any edition. For the Bible, book, chapter, and verse should all be cited, using periods for separation. The reference below is to Genesis, chapter 2, verse 1.

> According to the Christian myth of creation, at the end of the sixth day "the heavens and the earth were finished" (Gen. 2.1).

22. works in an anthology or book of readings: In the parenthetical reference for a work in an anthology, use the name of the author of the work, not that of the editor of the anthology. The page number, however, should be that found in the anthology. The following citation refers to an article by Frederic W. Gleach in an anthology edited by Jennifer Brown and Elizabeth Vibert.

> One of the essays in Brown and Vibert's collection argues that we should rethink the Pocahontas myth (Gleach 48).

In your list of Works Cited, this work should be alphabetized under Gleach, the author of the piece you have consulted, not under Brown. If you cite another work by a different author from the same anthology or book of readings, that should appear as a separate entry in your list of Works Cited—again, alphabetized under the author's name.

35b. ABOUT WORKS CITED

The Works Cited list in MLA style is an alphabetized list at the end of the essay, article, or book. It should include information about all the works you have cited. Unlike a Bibliography, however, a Works Cited list should not include works that you consulted but did not cite in the body of your text. The basic publication information of each entry in the list must include the work's publication medium (i.e., whether it appears in print, on the Web, on a CD, and so on).

1. single author: In most cases the Works Cited list is alphabetized by author last name. For a work with one author the entry should begin with the last name, followed by a comma, and then the author's first name or initials (use whatever appears on the work's title page), followed by a period. Entries for books then include the book's title, a period, and the publication information as it appears on the book's title and copyright pages; include the city of publication, a colon, the basic publisher's name (omit "Press," "Inc.," "Publisher," etc.), the copyright date, a period, and the publication medium. End every entry with a period.

> Frankfurt, Harry G. *The Importance of What We Care About: Philosophical Essays.* New York: Cambridge UP, 1988. Print.

2. two or three authors: Only the first author's name should be reversed. Note also that the authors' names should appear in the order they are listed; sometimes this is not alphabetical.

> Eagles, Munro, James P. Bickerton, and Alain Gagnon. *The Almanac of Canadian Politics.* Peterborough: Broadview, 1991. Print.

3. four or more authors: Either include all the authors' names or name only the first author followed by a comma and et al. (the abbreviation of the Latin *et alia*, meaning *and others*).

> Blais, Andre, et al. *Anatomy of a Liberal Victory.* Peterborough: Broadview, 2002. Print.

> Fromkin, Victoria, Robert Rodman, Neil Hultin, and Harry Logan. *An Introduction to Language.* 1st Canadian ed. Toronto: Harcourt, 1997.

Print.

4. corporate author: If a work has been issued by
a government body, a corporation, or some other organization and no author is identified, the entry should be
listed by the name of the group even if the group is also
the publisher. Note that corporate author entries for government documents begin with the name of the government; the various departments or agency subdivisions
then follow (e.g., Canada. Department of
Communications. Arts and Culture Branch.)

> Broadview Press. "Questions and Answers about
>   Book Pricing." *Broadview Press.* Broadview,
>   2008. Web. 17 Feb. 2005.
> Broadview Press. *2007 Annual Report.* Calgary:
>   Broadview, 2008. Print.
> Commonwealth of Massachusetts. "History of the
>   Arms and Great Seal of the Commonwealth of
>   Massachusetts." Public Records Division.
>   Commonwealth of Massachusetts, n.d. Web. 6
>   Oct. 2008.
> Ontario. Ministry of Natural Resources. Keeping the
>   Land: A Draft Land Use Strategy for the
>   Whitefeather Forest and Adjacent Areas.
>   Toronto: Queen's Printer for Ontario, 2005.
>   Print.

5. works with no author: Works with no author
should be alphabetized by title.

> *Sir Gawain and the Green Knight.* Trans. James
>   Winny. Peterborough: Broadview, 1992. Print.

6. two or more works by the same author:
The author's name should appear for the first entry only;
for subsequent entries substitute three hyphens for the
name of the author.

Menand, Louis. "Bad Comma: Lynne Truss's Strange
Grammar." Rev. of *Eats, Shoots and Leaves,* by
Lynne Truss. *The New Yorker* 28 June 2004: n.
pag. Web. 18 Feb. 2005.

---. *The Metaphysical Club: A Story of Ideas in
America.* New York: Knopf, 2002. Print.

7. edited works: If you are citing the parts of a
work written by an editor or editors, the entry should
begin with the names of the editor(s) and include the
abbreviation *ed.* or *eds.,* as follows:

Rosengarten, Herbert, and Amanda Goldrick Jones,
eds. *The Broadview Anthology of Poetry.* 2nd ed.
Peterborough: Broadview, 2008. Print.

When referring to an edited version of a work written by
another author or authors, list the editor after the title and
use the abbreviation "Ed." for "Edited by":

More, Thomas. *Utopia.* Ed. Paul Turner. London:
Penguin, 2003. Print.

8. works in translation: Entries for works in translation include the translator's name after the abbreviation
trans., as follows:

Calvino, Italo. *Cosmicomics.* 1965. Trans. William
Weaver. San Diego: Harvest-Harcourt, 1968.
Print.

**9. selections from anthologies or collections
of readings:** A selection from a collection of readings
or an anthology should be listed as follows below. If they
are available, be sure to add the selection's inclusive
page numbers after the anthology's publication date; if
there are no page numbers (as in many online sites),

write *n. pag.* for *no pagination.*

> Crawford, Isabella Valancy. "The Canoe."
> *Representative Poetry Online.* Ed. Ian Lancashire.
> n. pag. U of Toronto, Oct. 2002. Web. 17 Feb.
> 2005.
> Gleach, Frederic W. "Controlled Speculation:
> Interpreting the Saga of Pocahontas and Captain
> John Smith." *Reading Beyond Words: Contexts for
> Native History.* Eds. Jennifer S.H. Brown and
> Elizabeth Vibert. Peterborough: Broadview,
> 1996. 21–42. Print.
> Mahfouz, Naguib. "Half a Day." *The Picador Book of
> African Stories.* Ed. Stephen Gray. Basingstoke:
> Picador, 2001. 3–6. Print.

If you are listing two or more items from the same collection or anthology, create a full entry for the collection or anthology, then list each cited item in its own entry. Arrange the entries alphabetically by author, and use a short form for the collection or anthology, as in the following example:

> Brown, Jennifer S.H., and Elizabeth Vibert, eds.
> *Reading Beyond Words: Contexts for Native
> History.* Peterborough: Broadview, 1996. Print.
> Cruikshank, Julie. "Discovery of Gold on the
> Klondike: Perspectives from Oral Tradition."
> Brown and Vibert 433–59.
> Gleach, Frederic W. "Controlled Speculation:
> Interpreting the Saga of Pocahontas and Captain
> John Smith." Brown and Vibert 21–42.

10. multi-volume works: If you are citing two or more volumes of a multi-volume work, the entry should note the total number of volumes. If you cite only one of the volumes, list the volume cited after the title. If you wish, you may add the total number of volumes at the end of the entry, though MLA does not require this.

> Jeeves, Julie, ed. *A Reference Guide to Spanish
> Architecture.* 3 vols. Indianapolis: Hackett, 2005.
> Print.
>
> Mercer, Bobby, ed. *A Reference Guide to French
> Architecture.* Vol. 1. Indianapolis: Hackett, 2002.
> Print. 3 vols.

11. different editions: The edition should be specified whenever it is not the first edition. Include whatever the title page indicates about the particular edition, and use abbreviations (e.g., *rev. ed.* for *revised edition*, *2nd ed.* for *second edition*, and so on). Sometimes it may be helpful to specify editions more than once in a single entry—as, for example, with the second example below.

> Fowles, John. *The Magus.* Rev. ed. London: Jonathan
> Cape, 1977. Print.
>
> Shelley, Mary. *Frankenstein.* 1818 ed. Ed. Lorne
> Macdonald and Kathleen Scherf. 2nd Broadview
> ed. Peterborough: Broadview, 1999. Print.

12. reference work entries: List by the author of the entry, if known; otherwise, list by the entry itself. The citation of a well-known reference work (because such works are frequently updated) should not have full publication details; provide the edition number, date, and medium of publication only. Don't include page numbers for works that arrange their entries alphabetically.

> "Artificial." *Oxford English Dictionary.* 2nd ed. 1989.
> Print.
>
> Marsh, James. "Canoe, Birchbark." *The Canadian
> Encyclopedia.* 2000 ed. McClelland & Stewart,
> 1999. Print.
>
> "Saint Lawrence Seaway." *The Columbia
> Encyclopedia.* 6th ed. *Bartleby.com.* Bartleby,

2001. Web. 17 Feb. 2009.

13. works with a title in the title: The entries below follow the formatting guidelines specified in section G4.

> Bettelheim, Bruno. "'The Goose Girl': Achieving Autonomy." *The Uses of Enchantment: The Meaning and Importance of Fairy Tales.* 1976. Vintage Books ed. New York: Vintage-Random House, 1989. 136-43. Print.
> Morelli, Stefan. *Stoppard's* Arcadia *and Modern Drama.* London: Ashgate, 2004. Print.
> Wimsatt, C.W. *"Fern Hill" and British Poetry in the 1950s.* Toronto: ECW, 2004. Print.

14. material from prefaces, introductions, etc.: If you refer to something from a work's preface, introduction, or foreword, the reference under Works Cited should begin with the name of the author of that preface, introduction, or foreword. Add inclusive page numbers after the date of publication.

> Warkentin, Germaine. Introduction. *Set in Authority.* By Sara Jeannette Duncan. Peterborough: Broadview, 1996. 9–51. Print.

15. films, programs, interviews, performances, music, art: Films, radio or television programs, interviews, dramatic performances, musical recordings, and works of visual art should be listed as in the examples below.

FILMS, TELEVISION, RADIO, PERFORMANCES

> *Corner Gas.* CTV, 14 Feb. 2005. Television.
> *A Doll's House.* By Henrik Ibsen. Dir. Anthony Page.

Perf. Janet McTeer and Owen Teale. Belasco,
New York. 22 May 1997. Performance.

Bob Dylan. Concert. Wings Stadium, Kalamazoo. 8
Nov. 2008.

"Family Farm vs. Factory Farm." *Country Canada*.
CBC, 21 Nov. 2003. Radio. *CBC Archives*. Web.
17 Feb. 2005.

Wag the Dog. Dir. Barry Levinson. Perf. Robert
DeNiro and Dustin Hoffman. Alliance, 1997.
Film.

INTERVIEWS

Bellow, Saul. Interview. *Books in Canada* Sept. 1996:
2–6. Print.

Counts, Dorothy Ayers, and David R. Counts.
Interview. Pamela Wallin Live. CBC Newsworld.
26 Nov. 1997.

Rosengarten, Herbert. Personal interview. 21 Jan.
2009.

RECORDED MUSIC

Williams, Lucinda. "Real Love." *Little Honey*. Lost
Highway, 2008. CD.

WORKS OF VISUAL ART

Housser, Yvonne McKague. *Cobalt*. Oil on canvas.
1931. National Gallery of Canada, Ottawa.

16. magazine articles: The title of the article
should appear in quotation marks, the title of the magazine in italics. Note that no punctuation separates the
magazine name and the date of its publication, while a
colon is used to separate the date of publication from the
page reference. If no author is identified, the title of the
article should appear first.

MacRitchie, Lynn. "Ofili's Glittering Icons." *Art in America* Jan. 2000: 44–56. Print.
"Shifting Sands." *The Economist* 12–18 Feb. 2005: 46–47. Print.

If you accessed the article online yourself, you should include the date you accessed the source after the medium of publication (*Web*). If the website is hosted by a body other than the magazine itself, include the site name, sponsor, and date of posting (use *n.d.* if no date is listed) before the publication medium.

Gladwell, Malcolm. "The Art of Failure: Why Some People Choke and Others Panic." *The New Yorker* 21 Aug. 2000: n. pag. Web. 18 Feb. 2009.
MacRitchie, Lynn. "Ofili's Glittering Icons." Art in America Jan. 2000: n. pag. *Find Articles at BNET.* BNET. Web. 16 Feb. 2009.

17. newspaper articles: The basic principles to follow with newspaper articles or editorials are the same as with magazine articles (see above). Note, however, that when the newspaper's sections are paginated separately, section as well as page numbers are often required. If an article is not printed on consecutive pages, include only the first page number followed by a plus sign. In the following reference the article begins on page 12 of the first section:

Glanz, James. "Iraq's Shiite Alliance Wins Slim Majority in New Assembly." *New York Times* 17 Feb. 2005, sec. 1: 12+. Print.

If you are citing an online version of a newspaper article you should include the date you accessed the site as well as the site name.

Glanz, James. "Iraq's Shiite Alliance Wins Slim Majority in New Assembly." *New York Times* 17

Feb. 2005: n. pag. Web. 18 Feb. 2005.

18. journal articles: The basic principles are the same as with magazine articles, but entries for journal articles include the volume and issue numbers separated by a period.

> Roy, Indrani. "Irony and Derision in Congreve's *The Way of the World.*" *PMLA* 120.6 (2005): 60–72. Print.

If you are citing an online version of a journal article you should include the date you accessed the site as well as the site name. If the document is not paginated, write *n. pag.(not paginated)* in place of inclusive page numbers. Because printers don't always divide documents into the same number of pages, don't rely on the pagination of a printed hardcopy of the article as a guide.

> Sohmer, Steve. "12 June 1599: Opening Day at Shakespeare's Globe." *Early Modern Literary Studies* 3.1 (1997): n. pag. Web. 26 June 2008.

19. book reviews: The name of the reviewer (if it has been provided) should come first, followed by the title of the review (if there is one), and the information on the book itself, as follows:

> O'Hagan, Andrew. "In His Hot Head." Rev. of *Robert Louis Stevenson: A Biography*, by Claire Harman. *London Review of Books* 17 Feb. 2005: n. pag. *Arts and Letters Daily*. Chronicle of Higher Education, 2005. Web. 18 Feb. 2009.
> "Our Fathers." Rev. of *Please Don't Come Back from the Moon*, by Dean Bakopoulos. *The Economist* 1–18 Feb. 2005: 83. Print.
> Schuessler, Jennifer. "Family Values." Rev. of *The Love Wife*, by Gish Jen. *New York Review of*

Books 13 Jan. 2005: 16–17. Print.

20. periodical publications in online data-bases: Full newspaper, magazine, and journal articles are now often available in online databases subscribed to by the libraries of academic institutions. Begin the entries for such sources as you would if they were print publications, but omit the word *print*. If there is no pagination, use the abbreviation *n. pag.* in place of inclusive page numbers. End by providing the name of the database (in italics), *Web*, and the date of access.

> Citron, Paula. "A Journey into 'the Human Side of Dance.'" *Globe and Mail* 24 Sept. 2008: R4. *Canadian Newsstand.* Web. 6 Oct. 2008.
> Hill, Katherine C. "Virginia Woolf and Leslie Stephen: History and Literary Revolution." *PMLA* 96.3 (1981): 351-62. *JSTOR.* Web. 6 Oct. 2008.
> Pope, Charles. "Interior Bill Includes Funding for Arts, despite GOP Efforts to Avoid Controversial Issue." *CQ Weekly* 27 June 1998: 1771. *Academic Search Premier.* Web. 6 Oct. 2008.

21. online projects: In the case of large projects involving many contributors the name of the project should come first, not the name of the general editor:

> *Victorian Women Writers Project.* Ed. Perry Willett. Indiana U, May 2000. Web. 26 June 2002.

22. online books: As with all online references, you should provide date of access along with information as to author, publisher or hosting website, date of posting (if available), and so on. If the book also appears in a print version, it may be helpful to include the print publication information. For older works, the date alone is sufficient.

Emerson, Ralph Waldo. *The American Scholar.* 1837.
    Literary Works of American Transcendentalism.
    Ed. Ann Woodlief. Virginia Commonwealth U,
    1999. Web. 16 Mar. 2001.

Herman, Jonathan R. *I and Tao: Martin Buber's
    Encounter with Chuang Tzu.* Albany: State U of
    New York P, 1996. *NetLibrary.* Web. 5 Oct.
    2008.

Rinehart, Mary Roberts. *Tish.* 1916. Etext produced
    by Lynn Hill. *Project Gutenberg.* Project
    Gutenberg, 16 Feb. 2005. Web. 18 Feb. 2005.

23. information databases: You should provide
date of access as well as information about the source.

"Profile of Book Publishing and Exclusive Agency,
    for English Language Firms." Chart. *Statistics
    Canada,* 3 Mar. 2004. Web. 18 Feb. 2005.

24. publication on a CD-ROM or DVD-ROM:
Cite a work on CD-ROM or DVD-ROM as you would a
printed book, but omit print and add a description of the
medium of publication.

Beam, Kathryn L., and Traianos Gagos, eds. *The
    Evolution of the English Bible: From Papyri to
    King James.* Ann Arbor: U of Michigan P, 1997.
    CD-ROM.

25. posting to a discussion list: The date of the
posting as well as the date of access should be given.

Merrian, Joanne. "Spinoff: Monsterpiece Theatre."
    Online posting. 30 Apr. 1994. *Shaksper: The
    Global Electronic Shakespeare Conference.* Ed.
    Hardy M. Cook. Shaksper, 2007. Web. 23 Sept.
    2008.

26. electronic sources—other information: In the above pages information about electronic sources has been presented in an integrated fashion, with information about referencing hard copies of journal articles presented alongside information about referencing online versions, and so on. In general, begin an entry for an electronic source as you would an entry for a print publication, but leave out the designation *print*. Continue with the title of the website or database (in italics), the site publisher or sponsor, a comma, the date of posting (if there is no date listed, write *n.d.*), the medium of publication (*Web*), and the date on which you accessed the source. MLA does not require listing the site's URL, but if you feel that your readers would find your source more easily with the help of its electronic address, or if your instructor asks that it be included, put the Web address at the end of the entry in angle brackets, and follow it with a period. If your word processor automatically converts the address into a hyperlink, remove the hyperlink. An example of an entry that includes a URL is shown below. Notice that if a URL has to be divided, it must be broken only after a slash, with no hyphen to indicate the break.

Annis, Matthew. "The Fisher King." *Project Camelot*.
   U of Rochester, 2007. Web. 6 Oct. 2008.
   <http://www.lib.rochester.edu/camelot/
   Fisherking/fkessay.htm>.

ON THE WEB

A selection of complete essays in
MLA style may be found at
www.broadviewpress.com/writing.

35c. MLA STYLE SAMPLE

Following is a sample of text with citations in MLA style.

Urban renewal is as much a matter of psychology as it is of bricks and mortar. As Paul Goldberger has described, there have been many plans to revitalize Havana (50–61). But both that city and the community of Cuban exiles in Florida remain haunted by a sense of absence and separation. As Lourdes Casal reminds us, "Exile / is living where there is no house whatever / in which we were ever children" (lines 1–3).

The psychology of outsiders also makes a difference. Part of the reason Americans have not much noticed the dire plight of their fifth-largest city is that it does not stir the national imagination (Rybczynski 12). Conversely, there has been far more concern over the state of cities such as New Orleans and Quebec, whose history and architecture excite the romantic imagination. As Nora Phelps has discussed, the past is in itself a key trigger for romantic notions, and cities whose history is particularly visible will engender passionate attachments. And as Stephanie Wright and Carole King have detailed, almost all French-speaking Quebecers feel their heritage to be bound up with that of Quebec City (2: 171–74). (Richard Ford's character Frank Bascombe has suggested that "New Orleans defeats itself" by longing for "a mystery it doesn't have and never will, if it ever did" [48; ch. 3] but this remains a minority view.)

Georgiana Gibson is also among those who have investigated the interplay between urban psychology and urban reality (*Cities* 64–89). Gibson's personal website now includes a working model she is developing in an attempt to represent the effects of various psychological schemata on the landscape.

The above references connect to Works Cited as follows:

Works Cited

Casal, Lourdes. "Definition." Trans. Elizabeth Macklin. *The New Yorker* 26 Jan. 1998: 79. Print.

Ford, Richard. *The Sportswriter*. 1986. 2nd Vintage ed. New York: Vintage-Random House, 1995. Print.

Gibson, Georgiana. *Cities in the Twentieth Century*. Boston: Beacon, 2004. Print.

---. Homepage. *Geography. Brigham Young University*. Brigham Young U, 10 July 1999. Web. 30 June 2008.

Goldberger, Paul. "Annals of Preservation: Bringing Back Havana." *The New Republic* 26 Jan. 2005: 50–62. Print.

Phelps, Nora. "Pastness and the Foundations of Romanticism." *Romanticism on the Net* 11.3 (2007): n. pag. Web. 6 July 2008.

Rybczynski, Witold. "The Fifth City." Rev. of *A Prayer for the City*, by Buzz Bissinger. *The New York Review of Books* 5 Feb. 1998: 12–14. Print.

Wright, Stephanie, and Carole King. *Quebec: A History*. 2 vols. Montreal: McGill-Queen's UP, 2003. Print.

Among the details to notice:

- All important words in titles are capitalized.
- Dates appear in Works Cited only.
- Each source's medium of publication (e.g., *print*, *Web*) is included in Works Cited.
- Only the first author's first and last names are reversed in the list of Works Cited.

- If a book review or film review has a title, that should appear under Works Cited, which should also indicate the title of the book or film being reviewed.

- Translators should be included in Works Cited.

- Publisher as well as city of publication should be given.

- UP is the abbreviation used for University Press.

- Online citations include the date of publication or of last revision as well as the date of access.

- Where two or more works by the same author are included in Works Cited, second and subsequent entries substitute three hyphens and a period for the author name.

36. APA STYLE

There are two chief concerns when it comes to citing and documenting material: accuracy and consistency. Whatever system of citation is used, a research writer must follow it closely and consistently. Four of the most commonly used systems of citation are summarized in these pages—MLA style, APA style, Chicago style, and CSE style. The American Psychological Association (APA) style is used in many behavioural and social sciences.

It may also be helpful to consult exemplary essays. (A selection of these may be found on the Broadview Press website in the pages providing adjunct material to this and other Broadview writing texts; go to www.broadviewpress.com, and click on links.)

To understand more of the basic principles and workings of academic citation and documentation, students are advised to consult 34a Citation and Plagiarism and 34b Signal Phrases at the beginning of Chapter 34, pages 90–91.

36a. ABOUT IN-TEXT CITATIONS

1. in-text citation: The APA system emphasizes the date of publication, which must appear within an in-text citation. Whenever a quotation is given, the page number must also be provided:

> Bonnycastle (2007) refers to "the true and lively spirit of opposition" (p. 204) with which Marxist literary criticism invigorates the discipline.

It is common to mention the names of authors you are citing in the body of your text, as is done in the example above. If author names are not mentioned in the body of the text, however, they must be provided within the in-text citation:

> One overview of literary theory (Bonnycastle, 2007) has praised "the true and lively spirit of opposition" (p. 204) with which Marxist literary criticism invigorates the discipline.

If the reference does not involve a quotation (as it commonly does not in social science papers), only the date need be given as an in-text citation, providing that the author's name appears in the signal phrase:

> Bonnycastle (2007) argues that the oppositional tone of Marxist literary criticism invigorates the discipline.

A citation such as this connects to a list of references at the end of the paper. In this case the entry under "References" at the end of the paper would be as follows:

> Bonnycastle, S. (2007). *In search of authority: A guide to literary theory* (3rd ed.). Peterborough, ON: Broadview Press.

Notice here that the date of publication is again foregrounded, appearing immediately following the author's name. Notice too that all words in a title except the first word in the title, the first in the subtitle, and any proper nouns appear in lower case.

2. titles: italics/underlining/quotation marks: Notice in the above example that both the title and the subtitle are in italics. The APA allows either italics or underlining for titles. Most writers now seem to feel that italic type has a more attractive appearance than underlining does; that italics is the form used in published work (meaning that if you have used underlining and your work is then published, all that underlining has to be converted to italics); and that italics is just as easy as underlining to produce with word processing systems. For all those reasons, we use italics rather than underlining for titles in these pages.

3. titles of short works: The titles of works are not usually used in the body of the text. Titles of short works (such as articles, lyric poems, and short stories) should be put in quotation marks if they appear in the body of the text or in an in-text citation, with key words capitalized. (In the list of references, however, such works should *not* be put in quotation marks or italicized, and no words should be capitalized except the first word in the title and the first in the subtitle, if any.)

4. placing of in-text citations: The in-text citation comes directly after the name of the author or after the end quotation mark. Often, the citation comes just before the period or comma in the surrounding sentence. (If a quotation ends with punctuation other than a period or comma, then this should precede the end of the quotation, and a period or comma should still follow the parenthetical reference, if this is grammatically appropriate.)

The claim has been convincingly refuted by Ricks (2001), but it nevertheless continues to be put forward (Dendel, 2008).

One of Berra's favourite coaching tips was that "ninety per cent of the game is half mental" (Adelman, 2007, p. 98).

Berra at one point said to his players, "You can observe a lot by watching!" (Adelman, 2007, p. 98).

Garner (2005) associates statistics and pleasure.

5. parenthetical reference when text is in parentheses: If a parenthetical reference occurs within text in parentheses, commas are used to set off elements of the reference.

(See Figure 6.1 of Harrison, 2006, for data on transplant waiting lists.)

6. no signal phrase (or author not named in signal phrase): If the context does not make it clear who the author is, that information must be added to the in-text citation. Note that commas separate the name of the author, the date, and the page number (where this is given):

Even in recent years some have continued to believe that Marxist literary criticism invigorates the discipline with a "true and lively spirit of opposition" (Bonnycastle, 2007, p. 4).

7. electronic source—page number unavailable: If a Web document cited is in PDF format, the page numbers are stable and may be cited as one would the pages of a printed source. Many Web page numbers are unstable, however, and many more lack page numbers. In such cases you should provide a section or paragraph number if a reference is needed. For paragraphs APA suggests using either the abbreviation "para." or the symbol ¶. (Remember that with APA style you need only provide information as to author and date if you are not quoting directly.)

> In a recent Web posting a leading theorist has clearly stated that he finds such an approach "thoroughly objectionable" (Bhabha, 2005, para. 7).

> In a recent Web posting a leading theorist has clearly stated that he finds such an approach "thoroughly objectionable" (Bhabha, 2005, ¶ 7).

> Bhabha (2005) has clearly stated his opposition to this approach.

> Carter and Zhaba (2005) describe this approach as "more reliable than that adopted by Perkins" (Method section, para. 2).

If you are citing longer texts from electronic versions, chapter references may be more appropriate. For example, if the online Gutenberg edition of *Darwin's On the Origin of the Species* were being cited, the citation would be as follows:

> Darwin refers to the core of his theory as an "ineluctable principle" (1856, chap. 26).

Students should be cautioned that online editions of older or classic works are often unreliable; typically there are far more typos and other errors in such versions than there are in print versions.

8. two or more dates for a work: If you have consulted a re-issue of a work (whether in printed or electronic form), you should provide both the original date of publication and the date of the re-issue (the date of the version you are using).

Emerson (1837/1909) asserted that America's "long apprenticeship to the learning of other lands" was "drawing to a close" (para. 1).

The relevant entry in the list of references would look like this:

Emerson, R. W. (1909). *Essays and English Traits.* New York: P. F. Collier & Son. (Original work published 1837).

If you are citing work in a form that has been revised by the author, however, you should cite the date of the revised publication, not the original.

In a preface to the latest edition of his classic work (2004), Watson discusses its genesis.

9. multiple authors: If there are two or three authors, all authors should be named either in the signal phrase or in the in-text citation. Use *and* in the signal phrase but & in parentheses.

Chambliss and Best (2005) have argued that the nature of this research is practical as well as theoretical.

Two distinguished scholars have argued that the nature of this research is practical as well as theoretical (Chambliss & Best, 2005).

three to five authors: In the body of the text list the names of all authors the first time the work is referred to; for subsequent references use only the first author's name, followed by "et al." (short for the Latin *et alia*: *and others*).

Chambliss, Best, Didby, and Jones (2005) have
argued that the nature of this research is practical as
well as theoretical.

Four distinguished scholars have argued that the
nature of this research is practical as well as
theoretical (Chambliss, Best, Didby, & Jones, 2005).

more than five authors: Use only the first author's
name, followed by "et al." (short for the Latin *et alia*:
and others).

Chambliss et al. (2005) have argued that the nature
of this research is practical as well as theoretical.

Six distinguished scholars have argued that the
nature of this research is practical as well as
theoretical (Chambliss et al., 2005).

10. author unknown/corporate author: Be
sure to refer to the relevant organization and/or the title of
the piece so as to make the reference clear. For organiza-
tions, recommended practice is to provide the full name on
the first occasion, followed by an abbreviation, and then
to use the abbreviation for subsequent references:

Blindness has decreased markedly but at an uneven
pace since the late 1800s (National Institute for the
Blind [NIB], 2002).

11. electronic source—author not given: If the
author of the electronic source is not given, it may be
identified in the parenthetical reference by a short form
of the title.

The party's electronic newsletter said the candidate
mentioned his role in the protests ("Globalization,"
2004).

12. electronic source—date not given. Some electronic sources do not provide a date of publication. Where this is the case, use the abbreviation *n.d.* for *no date.*

> Some still claim that evidence of global warming is difficult to come by (Sanders, n.d.; Zimmerman, 2005).

13. order of authors' names: Works should appear in in-text citations in the same order they do in the list of references, i.e., alphabetically by author's last name and then by publication date.

> Various studies have established a psychological link between fear and sexual arousal (Aikens, Cox, & Bartlett, 1998; Looby, 1999a, 1999b, 2003; Looby & Cairns, 2008, in press).

> Various studies appear to have established a psychological link between fear and sexual arousal (Looby & Cairns, 1999, 2002, 2005).

14. two or more authors with the same last name: If the "References" list includes two or more authors with the same last name, the in-text citation should supply an initial:

> One of the leading economists of the time advocated wage and price controls (H. Johnston, 1977).

15. works in a collection of readings or anthology: In the in-text citation for a work in an anthology or collection of readings, use the name of the author of the work, not that of the editor of the anthology. If the work was first published in the collection you have consulted, there is only the one date to cite. But if the work is reprinted in that collection after having first been published elsewhere, cite the date of the original publication and the date of the collection you have consulted, separating these dates with a slash. The following citation refers to an article by Frederic W. Gleach that was first published in a collection of readings edited by Jennifer Brown and Elizabeth Vibert.

> One of the essays in Brown and Vibert's collection argues that we should rethink the Pocahontas myth (Gleach, 1996).

In your list of references, this work should be alphabetized under Gleach, the author of the piece you have consulted, not under Brown.

The next example is a lecture by George Simmel first published in 1903, which a student consulted in an edited collection by Roberta Garner that was published in 2001.

> Simmel (1903/2001) argues that the "deepest problems of modern life derive from the claim of the individual to preserve the autonomy and individuality of his existence" (p. 141).

The reference list entry would look like this:

> Simmel, G. (2001). The metropolis and mental life. In R. Garner (Ed.), *Social theory–Continuity and confrontation: A reader* (pp. 141–53). Peterborough, ON: Broadview Press. (Original work published in 1903).

As you can see, in your reference list these works are listed under the authors of the pieces (Gleach or Simmel), not under the compilers, editors, or translators of the collection (Brown & Vibert or Garner). If you cite another work by a different author from the same anthology or book of readings, that should appear as a separate entry in your list of works cited—again, alphabetized under the author's name.

16. indirect source: If you are citing a source from a reference other than the source itself, you should use the phrase "as cited in" (or a variation thereof) in your in-text citation.

> In de Beauvoir's famous phrase, "one is not born a woman, one becomes one" (as cited in Levey, 2001, para. 3).

In this case, the entry in your reference list would be for Levey, not de Beauvoir.

36b. ABOUT REFERENCES

The list of references in APA style is an alphabetized list at the end of the essay, article, or book. Usually, it includes all the information necessary to identify and retrieve each of the sources you have cited, and only the works you have cited. In this case the list is entitled *References*. If the list includes all works you have consulted, regardless of whether or not you have cited them, it should be entitled *Bibliography*.

1. single author: In most cases the references list is alphabetized by author last name. For a work with one author the entry should begin with the last name, followed by a comma, and then the author's initials as applicable, followed by the date of publication in parentheses. Note that initials are generally used rather than first names, even when authors are identified by first name in the work itself.

> Eliot, G. (2004). *Middlemarch: A study of provincial life* (G. Maertz, Ed.). Peterborough, ON: Broadview. (Original work published 1872).

132 The Broadview Pocket Guide to Writing

2. two or three authors: Last names should in all cases come first, followed by initials. Up to six authors may be listed in this way. Use an ampersand rather than *and* before the last author. Note that the authors' names should appear in the order they are listed; sometimes this is not alphabetical.

> Eagles, M., Bickerton, J. P., & Gagnon, A. (1991). *The almanac of Canadian politics.* Peterborough, ON: Broadview.

3. more than six authors: Rather than name all authors, name the first six and then use *et al.*

> Allain, P., Verny, C., Aubin, G., Pinon, K., Bonneau, D., Dubas, F., et al. (2005). Arithmetic word-problem-solving in Huntington's disease. *Brain and cognition, 57*(1), 1–3.

4. corporate author: If a work has been issued by a government body, a corporation, or some other organization and no author is identified, the entry should be listed by the name of the group.

> Broadview Press. (2005). *Annual report.* Calgary, AB: Author.
> Broadview Press. (n.d.). Questions and answers about book pricing. Broadview Press website. Retrieved from www.broadviewpress.com/bookpricing.asp?inc=bookpricing
> City of Toronto, City Planning Division. (2000, June). *Toronto at the crossroads: Shaping our future.* Toronto: Author.

5. works with no author: Works with no author should be alphabetized by title.

Columbia encyclopedia (6th ed.). (2001). New York:
    Columbia University Press.

If you have referred to only one entry in an
encyclopedia or dictionary, however, the entry in your
list of references should be by the title of that entry (see
below).

6. two or more works by the same author:
The author's name should appear for all entries. Entries
should be ordered by year of publication.

Menand, L. (2002). *The metaphysical club: A story of
    ideas in America.* New York: Knopf.
Menand, L. (2004, June 28). Bad comma: Lynne
    Truss's strange grammar. [Review of the book
    Eats, shoots & leaves]. *The New Yorker.* Retrieved
    from http://www.newyorker.com

If two or more cited works by the same author have
been published in the same year, arrange these
alphabetically and use letters to distinguish among them
(2005a), (2005b), and so on.

7. edited works: Entries for edited works include the
abbreviation *Ed.* or *Eds.*, as follows:

Gross, B., Field, D., & Pinker, L. (Eds.). (2002).
    New approaches to the history of psychoanalysis.
    New York: Duckworth.

**8. selections from anthologies or collections
of readings:** A selection from a collection of readings
or an anthology should be listed as follows:

Rosengarten, H. (2002). Fleiss's nose and Freud's
    mind: A new perspective. In B. Gross, D. Field,
    & L. Pinker (Eds.), *New approaches to the history
    of psychoanalysis* (pp. 232–243). New York:
    Duckworth.

Crawford, I. V. (n.d.). The canoe. *Representative poetry online*. Retrieved from http://www.eir.library.utoronto.ca/rpo/display/poem596

Gleach, F. W. (1996). Controlled speculation: Interpreting the saga of Pocahontas and Captain John Smith. In J. Brown & E. Vibert (Eds.), *Reading beyond words: Contexts for Native history* (pp. 21–42). Peterborough, ON: Broadview.

9. works available in both printed and electronic versions: If a work is available both online and in a printed journal, you are not required to provide the URL; if you have consulted the electronic version, however, that should be noted as follows.

Earn, B., & Towson, S. (2005). Shyness and aggression: A new study. *Journal of Personality and Social Psychology, 44*(3), 144–153. doi: 10.1006/jpsp.2005.0722

10. reference work entries: List by the author of the entry, if known; otherwise, list by the entry itself.

Marsh, J. (1999). "Canoe, birchbark." *The Canadian encyclopedia* (Year 2000 ed.). Toronto: McClelland & Stewart.

Saint Lawrence seaway. (2001). *The Columbia encyclopedia* (6th ed.). Retrieved from http://www.bartleby.com/65/st/STLawrSwy.html

11. films, programs, interviews, performances, music, art: Films, radio or television programs, interviews, dramatic performances, musical recordings, and paintings should be listed as follows:

Films, Television, Radio

Levinson, B. (Director). (1997). Wag the dog. [Motion picture]. Los Angeles: MGM.

Family farm vs. factory farm. (2003, November 23).
Country Canada. Toronto: CBC. *CBC Archives.*
Retrieved from http://www.archivescbc.ca/IDC-
I-73-1239-6930/pig_INDUSTRY/CLIP2

Interviews

Bellow, S. Interview. *Books in Canada.* Sept. 1996:
2–6.
Counts, D. A., & Counts, D. R. (1997, November
26). [Interview with Pamela Wallin]. *Pamela
Wallin Live.* CBC Newsworld.
Rosengarten, H. (2005, January 21). [Personal
interview].

12. magazine articles: Note that neither quotation
marks nor italics are used for the titles of articles. If no
author is identified, the title of the article should appear
first. If you are citing a printed version, you should give
the page reference for the article.

Gladwell, M. (2000, August 21). The art of failure:
Why some people choke and others panic. *The
New Yorker.* Retrieved from
http://www.gladwell.com/2000_08_21_a_
choking.htm
MacRitchie, L. (2000, January). Ofili's glittering
icons. *Art in America.* Retrieved from
http://www.findarticles.com.ofili.j672.jn.htm
Shifting sands. (2005, February 12–18). *The
Economist,* 46–47.

13. newspaper articles: The basic principles to follow with newspaper articles or editorials are the same as
with magazine articles (see above). Note that APA
requires that all page numbers for print versions be provided when articles do not continue on consecutive
pages.

Clash over Nobel cash. (1998, February 11). *The
    Washington Post*, A14.
Glanz, J. (2005, February 17). Iraq's Shiite alliance
    wins slim majority in new assembly. *The New
    York Times*, pp. A1, A12.

If you are citing an online version of a newspaper
article you have retrieved through a search of its
website, you should provide the URL for the site, not for
the exact location.

Glanz, J. (2005, February 17). Iraq's Shiite alliance
    wins slim majority in new assembly. *The New
    York Times*. Retrieved from
    http://www.nytimes.com

14. journal articles: The basic principles are the
same as with magazine articles. Volume number is considered part of the journal's title and should be italicized;
issue number is given in brackets for journals that are
paginated by issue. For online versions you should
include the digital object identifier (doi) where available,
as well as volume and issue number. If no doi is available you should cite a URL for the article (or for the
home page of the journal if the URL is very lengthy or if
the article is available by subscription only).

Barker, P. (2004). The impact of class size on the
    classroom behaviour of special needs students: A
    longitudinal study. *Educational Quarterly*, 25(4),
    87–99.
Hurka, T. M. (1996). Improving on perfectionism.
    Philosophical Review, 99, 462–473.
Roy, I. (2005). Irony as a psychological concept.
    American Psychologist, 58, 244–256. doi:
    10.1006/ap.2005.0680
Sohmer, S. (1999). Ways of perceiving maps and
    globes. *Current Research in Spatial Psychology*,

46(3). Retrieved from
http://www.shu.ac.uk/emls/03-1/sohmjuli.html

Surtees, P. (2008). The psychology of the children's crusade of 1212. *Studies in Medieval History and Society*, 3(4), 279–325. doi: 10.1008/smhs.2008.0581

15. book reviews: The name of the reviewer (if it has been provided) should come first, followed by the date and title of the review, and the information on the book itself, as follows:

O'Hagan, A. (2005, February 18). Fossil fuels. [Review of the book *Underground Energy*]. *London Review of Books*. Retrieved from http://www.lrb.co.uk/v27/n04/ohag01_.html

Our fathers. (2005, February 11–18). [Review of the book *Parenting: The other half*]. 83.

16. other Web references: In the case of online sources not covered by the above, the same principles apply. Where an author or editor is indicated, list by author. If the source is undated or its content likely to change, you should include the date on which you accessed the material.

Brown University. (2006, May). Brown University. Women writers project. Retrieved from http://www.brown.edu/

Profile of book publishing and exclusive agency, for English language firms [Chart]. (2002). *Statistics Canada*. Retrieved from http://www.statcan.ca/english/pgdb/arts02.htm

36c. APA STYLE SAMPLE

Following is a sample of text with citations in APA style. Note that a sample essay in APA style appears on the adjunct website associated with this book.

Urban renewal is as much a matter of psychology as it is of bricks and mortar. As Goldberger (2005) has described, there have been many plans to revitalize Havana. But both that city and the community of Cuban exiles in Florida remain haunted by a sense of absence and separation. As Lourdes Casal (1998) reminds us,

> Exile
>
> is living where there is no house whatever in which we were ever children; (1. 1–3)

The psychology of outsiders also makes a difference. Part of the reason Americans have not much noticed the dire plight of their fifth-largest city is that it does not "stir the national imagination" (Rybczynski, 1998, p. 12). Conversely, there has been far more concern over the state of cities such as New Orleans and Quebec, whose history and architecture excite the romantic imagination. As Nora Phelps (1998) has discussed, the past is in itself a key trigger for romantic notions, and it is no doubt inevitable that cities whose history is particularly visible will engender passionate attachments. And as Stephanie Wright and Carole King (2003) have detailed in an important case study, almost all French-speaking Quebecers feel their heritage to be bound up with that of Quebec City. (Richard Ford's character Frank Bascombe has suggested that "New Orleans defeats itself" by longing "for a mystery it doesn't have and never will, if it ever did" [Ford, 1995, 48] but this remains a minority view.)

Georgiana Gibson (2004a) is also among those who have investigated the interplay between urban psychology and urban reality. Gibson's personal website (2004b) now includes the first of a set of working models she is developing in an attempt to represent the effects of psychological schemata on the landscape.

The in-text citations above would connect to References as follows:

References

Casal, L. (1998, January 26). Definition. (E. Macklin, Trans.). *The New Yorker*, 79.

Ford, R. (1995). *The sportswriter* (2nd ed.). New York: Vintage-Random House.

Gibson, G. (2004a). *Cities in the twentieth century*. Boston: Beacon.

Gibson, G. (2004b, June 10). Homepage. Retrieved from http:www.geography.byu.edu/GIBSON/personal.htm

Goldberger, P. (2005, January 26). Annals of preservation: Bringing back Havana. *The New Yorker*, 50–62. Retrieved from http://www.newyorker.com

Phelps, N. (1998). Pastness and the foundations of romanticism. *Romanticism on the Net,* 11.3 doi: 10.1008/rotn.2007.4611

Rybczynski, W. (1998, February 5). The fifth city. [Review of the book *A prayer for the city*]. *The New York Review of Books*, 12–14.

Wright, S., & King, C. (2003). *Quebec: A history* (Vols. 1–2). Montreal: McGill-Queen's University Press.

Among the details to notice in this reference system:

- Where two or more works by the same author are included in References, they are ordered by date of publication.
- APA style prefers author initials rather than first names.
- Only the first words of titles and subtitles are capitalized, except for proper nouns.

- The date appears in parentheses near at the beginning of each entry in References.

- The in-text citation comes directly after the name of the author or after the end quotation mark. Often, these citations fall just before the period or comma in the surrounding sentence.

- If an in-text citation occurs within text in parentheses, commas are used to set off elements of the reference.

- When a work has appeared in an edited collection, information on the editors must be included in the reference.

- Authors' first and last names are reversed; note the use of the ampersand (&) between author names.

- Translators should be included under References.

- Publisher as well as city of publication should be given.

- Months and publisher names are not abbreviated; the day of the month follows the name of the month.

- Online references include the date of publication or of last revision in parentheses immediately after the author's name; note that, if a URL ends a reference entry, there is no period at the end of the entry.

37. CHICAGO STYLE

There are two chief concerns when it comes to citing and documenting material: accuracy and consistency. Whatever system of citation is used, a research writer must follow it closely and consistently. Four of the most commonly used systems of citation are summarized in these pages—MLA style, APA style, Chicago style, and CSE style.

It may also be helpful to consult exemplary essays. (A selection of these may be found on the Broadview Press website in the pages providing adjunct material to this and other Broadview writing texts; go to www.broadviewpress.com, and click on links.)

To understand more of the basic principles and workings of academic citation and documentation, students are advised to consult 34a. Citation and Plagiarism and 34b. Signal Phrases at the beginning of Chapter 34, pages 90–91.

The massively comprehensive *Chicago Manual of Style* provides full information both on an author-date system of citation that is similar to APA style, and to a traditional footnoting system. The latter is outlined below. A fuller outline is available in Kate Turabian's *A Manual for Writers of Term Papers, Theses, and Dissertations.*

The Chicago Manual of Style now deals extensively with the citation of electronic materials; sensibly, it recognizes that practices in such areas are likely to remain to some extent "under construction," and the editors emphasize that rules "are meant for the average case, and must be applied with a certain degree of elasticity."

1. footnoting: The basic principle of Chicago style is to create a footnote each time one cites a source:

> Bonnycastle refers to "the true and lively spirit of opposition" with which Marxist literary criticism invigorates the discipline.[1]

The superscript number [1] here is linked to the information provided where the same number appears at the foot of the page:

> 1. Stephen Bonnycastle, *In Search of Authority: An Introductory Guide to Literary Theory*, 3rd ed. (Peterborough: Broadview Press, 2007), 204.

If a full bibliography is included, Chicago Style now regards it as acceptable practice to use a shortened citation form such as the following:

Bonnycastle, *In Search of Authority*, 204.

All works cited (and works that have been consulted but are not cited in the body of your essay) must be included in a Bibliography that appears at the end of the essay. The reference under Bibliography at the end of the paper would in this case be as follows:

Bonnycastle, Stephen. *In Search of Authority: An Introductory Guide to Literary Theory.* 3rd ed. Peterborough: Broadview Press, 2007.

Notice in the above examples that the author's full first name is provided (not an initial). In a footnote, publication information is placed in parentheses, a page number for the quotation is provided, and the note is indented. In the entry in the Bibliography no parentheses are placed around the publication information, and the entry is out-dented.

2. titles: italics/underlining/quotation marks: Notice in the above example that both the title and the subtitle are in italics. Titles of short works (such as articles, poems, and short stories) should be put in quotation marks. In all titles key words should be capitalized.

3. when to include a citation: Any quotation should include a reference, as should factual information that is not general knowledge. Here is an example:

At the time of the rebellion per capita income is estimated to have been less than $500, and tens of thousands of children had already starved to death.[1]

The superscript number in the above text connects to a footnote as follows:

1. Sean Carver, "The Economic Foundations for Unrest in East Timor, 1970–1995," *Journal of Economic History* 21, no. 2 (2004): 103.

Note that where page numbers are unavailable it is recommended that other available information (such as paragraph or section references) be provided.

4. square brackets: If you need to include words of your own within a quotation, square brackets may be used for this purpose. Single quotation marks should be used for quotations within a quotation:

As Smith has pointed out, "it was [Raymond] Williams who first outlined the development in Britain of a 'print culture,' in his influential 1960s book *The Long Revolution*."[1]

If a quotation includes an error, or something the reader might assume to be an error, the word *sic* (Latin for *thus*) should be inserted in square brackets:

The secretary has written that "America, in it's [sic] wisdom, can be counted on to come to the assistance of those suffering under tyrannous regimes."[1]

5. multiple references to the same work: For later references to an already-cited source, use the author's last name, title, and page number only. (Note that the use of *op. cit.* is no longer accepted practice.)

1. Bonnycastle, *In Search of Authority*, 28.

If successive references are to the same work, use *ibid.* (an abbreviation of the Latin *ibidem*, meaning *in the same place*).

1. Sean Carver, "The Economic Foundations for Unrest in East Timor, 1970–1995," *Journal of Economic History* 21, no. 2 (2004): 103.
2. Ibid., 109.
3. Ibid., 111.
4. Jennifer Riley, "East Timor in the Pre-Independence Years," *Asian History Online* 11, no. 4 (2003): par. 18, http://www.aho.ubc.edu/prs/text-only/issue.45/16.3jr.txt.
5. Ibid., par. 24.

6. page number unavailable: If an Internet document cited is in PDF format, the page numbers are stable and may be cited in the same way that one would the pages of a printed book or journal article. Many Internet page numbers are unstable, however, and many more lack page numbers. Instead, provide a section number, paragraph number, or other identifier if available. Note that Chicago style now recommends (though it does not require) that date accessed be included for electronic sources.

2. Hanif Bhabha, "Family Life in 1840s Virginia," *Southern History Web Archives* (2003): par. 14. http://shweb.ut.edu/history/american.nineteenthc/bhabha.html (accessed March 3, 2009).

If you are citing longer texts from electronic versions, and counting paragraph numbers is impracticable, chapter references may be more appropriate. For example, if the online Gutenberg edition of Darwin's *On the Origin of Species* were being cited, the citation would be as follows:

Darwin refers to the core of his theory as an "ineluctable principle."[1]

1. Charles Darwin, *On the Origin of Species* (1856; Project Gutenberg, 2001), chap. 26, http://www.gutenberg.darwin.origin.frrp.ch26.html (accessed March 2, 2009).

Students should be cautioned that online editions of older or classic works are often unreliable; typically there are far more typos and other errors in online versions of literary texts than there are in print versions.

7. two or more dates for a work: Note that in the above example both the date of the original publication and the date of the modern edition are provided. If you are citing work in a form that has been revised by the author, however, you should cite the date of the revised publication, not the original.

1. Eric Foner, *Free Soil, Free Labor, Free Men: A Study of Antebellum America*, rev. ed. (New York: Oxford University Press, 1999), 178.

8. multiple authors: If there are two or three authors, they should be identified as follows in the footnote and in the Bibliography:

4. Eric Alderman and Mark Green, *Tony Blair and the Rise of New Labour* (London: Cassell, 2002), 180.

Alderman, Eric, and Mark Green. *Tony Blair and the Rise of New Labour*. London: Cassell, 2002.

Four or more authors: In the footnote name only the first author, and use the phrase *and others* (preferred to the Latin *et al.*); in the bibliography name all authors, as below:

11. Richard Johnston and others, *Letting the People Decide: Dynamics of a Canadian Election* (Montreal: McGill-Queen's University Press, 1992), 232.

Johnston, Richard, Andre Blais, Henry E. Brady, and Jean Crete. *Letting the People Decide: Dynamics of a Canadian Election.* Montreal: McGill-Queen's University Press, 1992.

9. author unknown/corporate author/ government document: Identify by the corporate author if known, and otherwise by the title of the work. Unsigned newspaper articles or dictionary and encyclopedia entries are usually not listed in the bibliography. In notes, unsigned dictionary or encyclopedia entries are identified by the title of the reference work, e.g., *Columbia Encyclopedia*, and unsigned newspaper articles are listed by the title of the article in footnotes but by the title of the newspaper in the bibliography. Ignore initial articles (the, a, an) when alphabetizing.

6. *National Hockey League Guide, 1966–67* (Toronto: National Hockey League, 1966), 77.
7. "Globalization's Effects Felt in Rural Ecuador," *New York Times*, September 12, 2004, A14.
8. Broadview Press, "Questions and Answers about Book Pricing," Broadview Press, http://www.broadviewpress.com/bookpricing.asp?inc=bookpricing (accessed March 5, 2009).
9. Commonwealth of Massachusetts, *Records of the Transportation Inquiry, 2004* (Boston: Massachusetts Publishing Office, 2005), 488.
10. Columbia Encyclopedia, "Ecuador," http://bartleby.com.columbia.txt.acc.html (accessed March 4, 2009).
11. House Committee on Ways and Means. Subcommittee on Trade, Free Trade Area of the

Americas: Hearings, 105th Cong., 1st sess., July
22, 1997, Hearing Print 105-32, 160,
http://www.waysandmeans.house.gov/hearings.asp
(accessed March 5, 2009).

Following are the bibliography entries for the preceding
notes:

Broadview Press. "Questions and Answers about
Book Pricing." Broadview Press.
http://www.broadviewpress.com/bookpricing.
asp?inc=bookpricing (accessed March 5, 2009).
Commonwealth of Massachusetts. *Records of the
Transportation Inquiry, 2004.* Boston:
Massachusetts Publishing Office, 2005.
National Hockey League Guide, 1966-67. Toronto:
National Hockey League, 1966.
New York Times. "Globalization's Effects Felt in Rural
Ecuador," September 12, 2004, A14.
U.S. Congress. House Committee on Ways and
Means. Subcommittee on Trade. *Free Trade Area
of the Americas: Hearing before the Subcommittee
on Trade.* 105th Cong., 1st sess., July 22, 1997.
Hearing Print 105-32.
http://www.waysandmeans.house.gov/
hearings.asp (accessed July 22, 2009).

**10. works from a collection of readings or
anthology:** In the citation for a work in an anthology
or collection of essays, use the name of the author of the
work you are citing. If the work is reprinted in one
source but was first published elsewhere, include the
details of the original publication in the bibliography.

6. Eric Hobsbawm, "Peasant Land Occupations," in
Uncommon People: Resistance and Rebellion
(London: Weidenfeld & Nicolson, 1998), 167.
7. Frederic W. Gleach, "Controlled Speculation:

Interpreting the Saga of Pocahontas and Captain John Smith," in *Reading Beyond Words: Contexts for Native History*, 2nd ed., ed. Jennifer Brown and Elizabeth Vibert (Peterborough: Broadview Press, 2003), 43.

Gleach, Frederic W. "Controlled Speculation: Interpreting the Saga of Pocahontas and Captain John Smith." In *Reading Beyond Words: Contexts for Native History*, 2nd ed., edited by Jennifer Brown and Elizabeth Vibert. Peterborough: Broadview Press, 2003: 39–74.

Hobsbawm, Eric. "Peasant Land Occupations." In *Uncommon People: Resistance and Rebellion*. London: Weidenfeld & Nicolson, 1998: 166–190. Originally published in *Past and Present* 62 (1974): 120–152.

11. indirect source: If you are citing a source from a reference other than the source itself, you should include information about both sources, supplying as much information as you are able to about the original source.

In de Beauvoir's famous phrase, "one is not born a woman, one becomes one."[1]

1. Simone de Beauvoir, *The Second Sex* (London: Heinemann, 1966), 44, quoted in Ann Levey, "Feminist Philosophy Today," *Philosophy Now*, par. 8, http://www.ucalgary.ca.philosophy. nowsite675.html (March 4, 2005).

de Beauvoir, Simone. *The Second Sex*. London: Heinemann, 1966. Quoted in Ann Levey, "Feminist Philosophy Today," *Philosophy Now*, http://www.ucalgary.ca.philosophy.nowsite675. html (accessed March 4, 2005).

12. two or more works by the same author:
After the first entry in the bibliography, use three hyphens for subsequent entries of works by the same author (rather than repeat the author's name). Entries for multiple works by the same author are normally arranged alphabetically by title.

> Menand, Louis. *The Metaphysical Club: A Story of Ideas in America*. New York: Knopf, 2002.
> ---. "Bad Comma: Lynne Truss's Strange Grammar." *The New Yorker*, June 28, 2004. http://www.Newyorker.com/critics/books/?0406 28crbo_books1 (accessed March 5, 2009).

13. edited works: Entries for edited works include the abbreviation *ed.* or *eds.* Note that when ed. appears after a title, it means "edited by."

> 5. Brian Gross, ed., *New Approaches to Environmental Politics: A Survey* (New York: Duckworth, 2004), 177.
> 6. Mary Shelley, *Frankenstein*, 2nd ed., ed. Lorne Macdonald and Kathleen Scherf, Broadview Edition (1818; Peterborough: Broadview Press, 2001), 89.

> Gross, Brian, ed. *New Approaches to Environmental Politics: A Survey*. New York: Duckworth, 2004.
> Shelley, Mary. *Frankenstein*. 2nd ed. Edited by Lorne Macdonald and Kathleen Scherf. Broadview Edition. Peterborough: Broadview, 2001. First published in 1818.

14. magazine articles: The titles of articles appear in quotation marks. The page range should appear in the bibliography if it is known. (This will not always be possible if the source is an electronic version.) If no authorship is attributed, list the title of the article as the "author" in the footnote, and the magazine title as the "author" in the bibliography.

2. Lynn MacRitchie, "Ofili's Glittering Icons," *Art in America*, January 2000, par. 14, http://www.findarticles.com.ofili.j672.jn.htm (accessed March 4, 2009).

3. "Shifting Sands," *Economist*, February 12-18, 2005, 47.

4. Malcolm Gladwell, "The Art of Failure: Why Some People Choke and Others Panic," *The New Yorker*, August 21, 2000, par 8, http://www.gladwell.com/2000_08_21_a_choking .html (accessed March 5, 2009).

Economist. "Shifting Sands." February 12–18, 2005, 46–47.

Gladwell, Malcolm. "The Art of Failure: Why Some People Choke and Others Panic." *The New Yorker*, August 21, 2000. http://www.gladwell.com/2000_08_21_a_ choking.html (accessed March 5, 2009).

MacRitchie, Lynn. "Ofili's Glittering Icons." *Art in America*, January 2000, 75–84. http://www.findarticles.com.ofili.j672.jn.htm. (accessed March 4, 2009).

15. newspaper articles: The basic principles to follow with newspaper articles or editorials are the same as with magazine articles (see above). Page numbers should be given if your source is a hard copy or microfilm rather than an electronic version.

1. "Clash over Nobel Cash," *Washington Post*, February 11, 1998, A14.

2. Glanz, Jane, "Iraq's Shiite Alliance Wins Slim Majority in New Assembly," *New York Times*, February 17, 2005, http://www.nytimes.com/2005/02/17/ international/middleeast/17cnd-iraq.html (accessed March 4, 2005).

Glanz, Jane. "Iraq's Shiite Alliance Wins Slim
Majority in New Assembly." *New York Times*,
February 17, 2005.
http://www.nytimes.com/2005/02/17/internationa
l/middleeast/17cnd-iraq.html (accessed March 4,
2005).

Washington Post. "Clash over Nobel Cash." February
11, 1998, A14.

16. journal articles: The basic principles are the
same as with magazine articles. Volume number should
not be italicized; issue number as well as page number
should be provided where available.

1. Paul Barker, "The Impact of Class Size on the
Classroom Behavior of Special Needs Students: A
Longitudinal Study," *Educational Quarterly* 25, no.
4 (2004): 88.
2. Thomas Hurka, "Improving on Perfectionism,"
Philosophical Review 99 (1996): 472.
3. Peter Surtees. "The Psychology of the Children's
Crusade of 1212," *Studies in Medieval History and
Society* 3, no. 4 (2009): 303.
4. Sally Sohmer, "Ways of Perceiving Maps and
Globes," *Psychology and History* 3, no. 4 (2004):
par. 7, http://www.shu.ac.uk/emls/03-
1/sohmjuli.html (accessed March 5, 2005).

Barker, Paul. "The Impact of Class Size on the
Classroom Behavior of Special Needs Students:
A Longitudinal Study." *Educational Quarterly*
25, no. 4 (2004): 87–99.
Hurka, Thomas M. "Improving on Perfectionism."
Philosophical Review 99 (1996): 462–73.
Surtees, Peter. "The Psychology of the Children's
Crusade of 1212." *Studies in Medieval History
and Society* 3, no. 4 (2009): 279–304.

Sohmer, Sally. "Ways of Perceiving Maps and
Globes." *Psychology and History* 3, no. 4 (2004).
http://www.shu.ac.uk/emls/03-1/sohmjuli.html
(accessed March 5, 2005).

**17. films, programs, interviews, perfor-
mances, music, art:** Films, radio or television programs, interviews, dramatic performances, musical
recordings, and paintings should be listed as follows:

Films, Television, Radio

1. *Wag the Dog*, directed by Barry Levinson (Los
   Angeles: MGM, 1997).
2. Charles White, *Dr. Rock*, Radio York, July 2,
   2006.

Wag the Dog. Directed by Barry Levinson. Los
Angeles: MGM, 1997.
White, Charles. Dr. Rock. Radio York, July 2, 2006.

Interviews

1. Saul Bellow, interview by Jim Smith, *Books in
   Canada*, September 1996, 3.
2. Dorothy Counts and David Counts, interview by
   Pamela Wallin, *Pamela Wallin Live*, CBC
   Television, November 26, 2002.
3. Herbert Rosengarten, telephone interview by
   author, January 21, 2005.

Bellow, Saul. Interview by Jim Smith. *Books in
Canada*, September 1996, 2–6.
Counts, Dorothy and David Counts. Interview by
Pamela Wallin. *Pamela Wallin Live.* CBC
Television, November 26, 2002.
Rosengarten, Herbert. Telephone interview by
author. January 21, 2005.

Note that unpublished interviews and unattributed interviews are usually not included in the bibliography.

18. book reviews: The name of the reviewer (if it has been provided) should come first, as shown below:

1. Andrew O'Hagan, "Fossil Fuels," review of *Underground Energy*, by Phyllis Jackson, *London Review of Books*, February 18, 2005, http://www.lrb.co.uk/v27/n04/ohag01_.html (accessed March 5, 2009).

O'Hagan, Andrew. "Fossil Fuels." Review of *Underground Energy*, by Phyllis Jackson. *London Review of Books*, February 18, 2005. http://www.lrb.co.uk/v27/n04/ohag01_.html (accessed March 5, 2009).

19. other Web references: In the case of online sources not covered by the above, the same principles apply. Where an author or editor is indicated, list by author.

Brown University. *Women Writers Project.* http://www.brown.edu/~letrs/html (accessed March 5, 2009).
"Profile of book publishing and exclusive agency, for English language firms, 2004." *Statistics Canada.* http://www40.statcan.ca/101/cst01/arts02.htm (accessed March 6, 2009).

37a. CHICAGO STYLE SAMPLE

A sample of text with citations in Chicago style appears on the following page. Note that a sample essay in Chicago style appears on the adjunct website associated with this book.

Urban renewal is as much a matter of psychology as it is of bricks and mortar. As Paul Goldberger has described, there have been many plans to revitalize Havana.[1] But both that city and the community of Cuban exiles remain haunted by a sense of absence and separation.

The psychology of outsiders also makes a difference. Part of the reason Americans have not much noticed the dire plight of their fifth-largest city is that it does not "stir the national imagination."[2] Conversely, there has been far more concern over the state of cities such as New Orleans and Quebec that excite the romantic imagination. Nora Phelps' work discusses how cities whose history is particularly visible engender passionate attachments; for example, almost all French-speaking Quebecers feel their heritage to be bound up with that of Quebec City. (Richard Ford's character Frank Bascombe has suggested that "New Orleans defeats itself" by longing "for a mystery it doesn't have,"[3] but this remains a minority view.)

Georgiana Gibson has investigated the interplay between urban psychology and urban reality, and her website includes the first of a set of

1 Paul Goldberger, "Annals of Preservation: Bringing Back Havana," *The New Republic*, January 2005, 54.
2 Witold Rybczynski, "The Fifth City," review of *A Prayer for the City*, by Buzz Bissinger, *New York Review of Books*, February 5, 1998, 13.
3 Richard Ford, *The Sportswriter*, 2nd ed. (New York: Vintage-Random House, 1995), 48.

The bibliography relating to the above text would be as follows:

Bibliography

Ford, Richard. *The Sportswriter.* 2nd ed. New York: Vintage-Random House, 1995.

Gibson, Georgiana. *Cities in the Twentieth Century.* Boston: Beacon, 2004.

---. Homepage. http:www.geography.by/ u.edu/GIBSON/personal.htm (accessed March 4, 2009).

Goldberger, Paul. "Annals of Preservation: Bringing Back Havana." *New Yorker,* January 26, 2005, 50–62. http://www.findarticles.com.goldberg.p65.jn.htm (accessed March 4, 2009).

Phelps, Nora. "Pastness and the Foundations of Romanticism." *Romanticism on the Net* 11.3 (May 2007). http://users.ox.ac.uk/-scat0385/phelpsmws.htm (accessed March 4, 2009).

Rybczynski, Witold. "The Fifth City." Review of *A Prayer for the City,* by D.B. Smith. *New York Review of Books,* February 5, 1998, 12-14.

Among the details to notice in this reference system:

- Where two or more works by the same author are included in the bibliography, they are normally arranged alphabetically by title.

- All major words in titles and subtitles are capitalized.

- Date of publication must appear, where known. Provision of your date of access to electronic materials may be helpful, but is not required.

- Commas are used to separate elements within a footnote, and, in many circumstances, periods separate these same elements in the bibliographic entry.

- When a work has appeared in an edited collection, information on the editors must be included in the reference.

- First authors' first and last names are reversed in the bibliography.

- Translators must be noted both in footnotes and in the bibliography.

- Publisher as well as city of publication should be given.

- Months and publisher names are not abbreviated.

- The day of the month comes after the name of the month.

- Online references should not include the revision date but may include the date on which you visited the site (access date).

38. CSE STYLE

There are two chief concerns when it comes to citing and documenting material: accuracy and consistency. Whatever system of citation is used, a research writer must follow it closely and consistently. Four of the most commonly used systems of citation are summarized in these pages—MLA style, APA style, Chicago style, and CSE (Council of Science Editors) style. It may also be helpful to consult exemplary essays. (A selection of these may be found on the Broadview Press website associated with this book: www.broadviewpress.com/writing.)

To understand more of the basic principles and workings of academic citation and documentation, students are advised to consult 34a. Citation and Plagiarism and 34b. Signal Phrases at the beginning of Chapter 34, pages 90–91.

The Council of Science Editors (CSE) style of documentation is commonly used in the natural sciences and the physical sciences. Guidelines are set out in *The CSE Manual for Authors, Editors, and Publishers*, 7th ed. (2006).

1. in-text citation: Citations in CSE style may follow three alternative formats: a citation-name format, a citation-sequence format, or a name-year format.

a. In the citation-name format, a reference list is compiled and arranged alphabetically by author. Each reference is then assigned a number in sequence, with the first alphabetical entry receiving the number 1, the second the number 2, and so on. Whenever you refer in your text to the reference labelled with number 3, for example, you use either a superscript number 3 (in one variation) or the same number in parentheses (in another).

> The difficulties first encountered in this experiment have been accounted for, according to Zelinsky[3]. However, the variables still have not been sufficiently well controlled for this type of experiment, argues Gibson[1].

The difficulties first encountered in this experiment have been accounted for, according to Zelinsky (3). However, the variables still have not been sufficiently well controlled for this type of experiment, argues Gibson (1).

b. In the citation-sequence format, superscript numbers (or numbers in parentheses) are inserted after the mention of any source. The first source mentioned receives number 1, the second number 2, and so on.

The difficulties first encountered in this experiment have been accounted for, according to Zelinsky[1]. However, the variables still have not been sufficiently well controlled for this type of experiment, argues Gibson[2].

The difficulties first encountered in this experiment have been accounted for, according to Zelinsky (1). However, the variables still have not been sufficiently well controlled for this type of experiment, argues Gibson (2).

Reuse the number you first assign to a source whenever you refer to it again.

c. In the name-year format, you cite the author name and year of publication in parentheses:

The key contributions to the study of variables in the 1990s (Gibson et al. 1998; Soames 1999; Zelinsky 1997) have been strongly challenged in recent years.

2. list of references: Citations in CSE style must correspond to items in a list of References. In the citation-name format, entries are arranged alphabetically and assigned a number.

1. Gibson DL, Lampman GM, Kriz FR, Taylor DM.
   Introduction to statistical techniques in the
   sciences. 2nd ed. New York: MacQuarrie
   Learning; 1998. 1254 p.
2. Soames G. Variables in large database experiments.
   J Nat Hist. 1999;82: 1811–41.
3. Zelinsky KL. The study of variables: an overview.
   New York: Academic; 1997. 216 p.

In the citation-sequence format, the references are listed
in the sequence in which they have been cited in the
text.

1. Zelinsky KL. The study of variables: an overview.
   New York: Academic; 1997. 216 p.
2. Gibson DL, Lampman GM, Kriz FR, Taylor DM.
   Introduction to statistical techniques in the
   sciences. 2nd ed. New York: MacQuarrie
   Learning; 1998. 1254 p.
3. Soames G. Variables in large database experiments.
   J Nat Hist. 1999;82: 1811–41.

In the name-year format, the references are listed
alphabetically, and the year of publication is given
prominence.

Gibson DL, Lampman GM, Kriz FR, Taylor DM.
       1998. Introduction to statistical techniques in
       the sciences. 2nd ed. New York: MacQuarrie
       Learning. 1254 p.
Soames G. 1999. Variables in large database
       experiments. J Nat Hist. 82: 1811–41.
Zelinsky KL. 1997. The study of variables: an
       overview. New York: Academic. 216 p.

The basic principles of the system are the same
regardless of whether one is citing a book, an article in
a journal or magazine, a newspaper article, or an
electronic document.

38a. CSE STYLE SAMPLE

Over the centuries scientific study has evolved into several distinct disciplines. Physics, chemistry, and biology were established early on; in the nineteenth and twentieth centuries they were joined by others, such as geology and ecology. Much as the disciplines have their separate spheres, the sphere of each overlaps those of others. This may be most obvious in the case of ecology, which some have claimed to be a discipline that makes a holistic approach to science respectable[1]. In the case of geology, as soon as it became clear in the nineteenth century that the fossil record of geological life would be central to the future of geology, the importance of connecting with the work of biologists became recognized[2]. Nowadays it is not surprising to have geological research conducted jointly by biologists and geologists (e.g., the work of Newton, Trewman, and Elser[3]). And, with the acceptance of "continental drift" theories in the 1960s and 1970s, physics came to be increasingly relied on for input into discussions of such topics as collision tectonics (e.g., Pfiffton, Earn, and Brome[4]).

The growth of the subdiscipline of biochemistry at the point of overlap between biology and chemistry is well-known, but many are unaware that the scope of biological physics is almost as broad; Frauenfrommer[5] provides a helpful survey. Nowadays it is not uncommon, indeed, to see research such as the recent study by Corel, Marks, and Hutner[6], or that by Balmberg, Passano, and Proule[7], both of which draw on biology, chemistry, and physics simultaneously.

Interdisciplinary scientific exploration has also been spurred by the growth of connections between the pure sciences and applied sciences such as meteorology, as even a glance in the direction of recent research into such topics as precipitation[8] or crating[9] confirms. But to the extent that science is driven by the applied, will it inextricably become more and more driven by commercial concerns? Christopher Haupt-Lehmann[10] thinks not.

The citations above would connect to References as follows:

References

1. Branmer A. Ecology in the twentieth century: a history. New Haven: Yale UP; 2004. 320 p.
2. Lyell C. Principles of geology. London: John Murray; 1830. 588 p.
3. Newton MJ, Trewman NH, Elser S. A new jawless invertebrate from the Middle Devonian. Paleontology 2004; 44 (1):43–52. http://www.onlinejournals.paleontology.44/html (accessed March 5, 2009).
4. Pfiffton QA, Earn PK, Brome C. Collision tectonics and dynamic modelling. Tectonics 2000;19(6):1065–94.
5. Frauenfrommer H. Introduction. Frauenfrommer H, Hum G, Glazer RG, editors. Biological physics third international symposium; 1998 Mar 8–9; Santa Fe, NM [Melville, NY]: American Institute of Physics. 386 p.
6. Corel B, Marks VJ, Hutner H. The modelling effect of Elpasolites. Chemical Sciences 2009;55(10):935–38.
7. Balmberg NJ, Passano C, Proule AB. The Lorenz-Fermi-Pasta-Ulam experiment. Physica D: Nonlinear phenomena [serial online] 2005; 138(1):1–43. Available at http://www.elseviere.com/locate/phys (accessed March 21, 2009).
8. Caine JS, Gross SM, Baldwin G. Melting effect as a factor in precipitation-type forecasting. Weather and Forecasting 2000;15(6):700–14.
9. Pendleton AJ. Gawler cration. Regional Geology 2001;11:999–1016.
10. Haupt-Lehmann C. Money and science: the latest word. New York Times 2001 Mar 23; Sect. D:22(col 1).

Among the details to notice in the citation-sequence format of the CSE style are the following:

- The entries in References are listed in the order they first appear in the text.

- Unpunctuated initials rather than first names are used in References.

- The date appears near the end of the reference, before any page reference.

- Only the first words of titles are capitalized (except for proper nouns and the abbreviated titles of journals).• When a work has appeared in an edited collection the names of the editor(s) as well as the author(s) must appear in the reference.

- *and* is used for in-text citations of works with more than one author—but not in the corresponding reference.

- Publisher as well as city of publication should be given.

- Months and journal names are generally abbreviated.

- References to electronic publications include the date of access as well as date of publication or latest revision.

- Names of articles appear with no surrounding quotation marks; names of books and journal titles appear with no italics.

On the next page, the same passage appears with the CSE name-year format used:

Over the centuries scientific study has evolved into several distinct disciplines. Physics, chemistry, and biology were established early on; in the nineteenth and twentieth centuries, they were joined by others, such as geology and ecology. Much as the disciplines have their separate spheres, the sphere of each overlaps those of others. This may be most obvious in the case of ecology, which some have claimed to be a discipline that makes a holistic approach to science respectable (Branmer 2004). In the case of geology, as soon as it became clear in the nineteenth century that the fossil record of geological life would be central to the future of geology, the importance of connecting with the work of biologists became recognized (Lyell 1830). Nowadays it is not surprising to have geological research conducted jointly by biologists and geologists (e.g., Newton, Trewman, and Elser 2001). And, with the acceptance of "continental drift" theories in the 1960s and 1970s, physics came to be increasingly relied on for input into discussions of such topics as collision tectonics (e.g., Pfiffton, Earn, and Brome 2000).

The growth of the subdiscipline of biochemistry at the point of overlap between biology and chemistry is well-known, but many are unaware that the scope of biological physics is almost as broad; Frauenfrommer

(1998) provides a helpful survey. Nowadays it is not uncommon, indeed, to see research such as the recent study by Corel, Marks, and Hutner (2009) or that by Balmberg, Passano, and Proule (2005), both of which draw on biology, chemistry, and physics simultaneously.

Interdisciplinary scientific exploration has also been spurred by the growth of connections between the pure sciences and applied sciences such as meteorology, as even a glance in the direction of recent research into such topics as precipitation (Caine, Gross, and Baldwin 2000) or crating (Pendleton 2001) confirms. But to the extent that science is driven by the applied, will it inextricably become more and more driven by commercial concerns? Christopher Haupt-Lehmann (2001) thinks not.

The citations above would connect to References as follows:

References

Branmer A. 2004. Ecology in the twentieth century: a history. New Haven: Yale UP. 320 p.

Balmberg NJ, Passano C, Proule AB. 2005. The Lorenz-Fermi-Pasta-Ulam experiment. Physica D: Nonlinear phenomena [serial online]. 138(1):1–43. Available at the Elsevier Journals website via the Internet (http://www.elseviere.com/locate/phys).

Caine JS, Gross SM, Baldwin G. 2000. Melting effect as a factor in precipitation-type forecasting. Weather and Forecasting. 15(6):700–14.

Corel B, Marks VJ, Hutner H. 2009. The modelling effect of Elpasolites. Chem Sci. 55(10):935–38.

Frauenfrommer H. Introduction. Frauenfrommer H, Hum G, Glazer RG, editors. 1998 Mar 8-9. Biological physics third international symposium. Santa Fe, NM. [Melville, NY]: American Institute of Physics. 386 p.

Haupt-Lehmann C. 2001 Mar 23. Money and science: the latest word. New York Times; Sect D:22 (col 2).

Lyell C. 1830. Principles of geology. London: John Murray. 588 p.

Newton MJ, Trewman NH, Elser S. 2001. A new jawless invertebrate from the Middle Devonian. Paleontology. 44 (1):43–52. Available from the Online journals site via the Internet (http://www.onlinejournals.paleontology.44/html).

Pendleton AJ. 2001. Gawler cration. Reg Geol; 11:999–1016.

Pfiffton QA, Earn PK, Brome C. 2000. Collision tectonics and dynamic modelling. Tectonics. 19(6):1065–94.

Among the details to notice in this reference system are the following:

- The entries in References are listed in alphabetical order by author.

- Unpunctuated initials rather than first names are used in References.

- The date appears immediately after the author name(s) at the beginning of the reference, before any page reference.

- The in-text citation comes before the period or comma in the surrounding sentence.

- Only the first words of titles are capitalized (except for proper nouns and the abbreviated titles of journals).

- When a work has appeared in an edited collection the names of the editor(s) as well as the author(s) must appear in the reference.

- *and* is used for in-text citations of works with more than one author—but not in the corresponding reference list entry.

- Publisher as well as city of publication should be given.

- Months and journal names are generally abbreviated.

- References to electronic publications include the date of publication or latest revision.

- Names of articles appear with no surrounding quotation marks; names of books, journals, etc. appear with no italics.

39. RESEARCH IN VARIOUS DISCIPLINES

39a. ANTHROPOLOGY

Citation and Documentation

The American Anthropology Association publishes its own brief Style Guide. In almost all particulars it follows the Chicago Style of parenthetical citation. It does, however, make some exceptions, most notably in using a colon (rather than a comma) to separate date and page number in a parenthetical citation:

> Evidence now suggests that the kinship system of the Pacaa Nova is extraordinarily complex (Von Graeve 2007: 24–35).

The AAA Style Guide may be downloaded from the AAA website.

Some Useful Websites

American Anthropological Association

www.aaanet.org   The official site of the AAA includes a range of useful information, as well as many useful links.

Anthropology Research on the Internet

www.archeodroit.net/anthro   This site, with an emphasis on archaeology, includes links to a great deal of useful information.

JSTOR

www.jstor.org   Founded in 1995 as a not-for-profit organization, this site is a leader in providing electronic access to a wide variety of scholarly journals online.

Some Respected Journals

American Anthropologist   The flagship journal of the

American Anthropology Association Also available through JSTOR.

American Ethnologist A respected journal published by the American Anthropological Association.

Annual Review of Anthropology Provides helpful reviews and syntheses of recent literature in the discipline.

Anthropologica The official journal of the Canadian Anthropological Society.

Anthropology Today A bi-monthly journal, aimed at the general public as well as at anthropologists and students.

Australian Journal of Anthropology This respected journal is published by the Australian Anthropological Society.

Cultural Anthropology A leading journal published by the American Anthropological Association.

Journal of the Royal Anthropological Society (formerly *Man*) The most established British journal in the discipline.

39b. ART HISTORY

Citation and Documentation

Art history and other disciplines in the Fine Arts generally use MLA style; For details see the section above.

Some Useful Websites

Association of Art Historians

www.aah.org The largest British association in this discipline maintains a helpful website.

College Art Association

www.collegeart.org   This is the main site for America's umbrella association of art historians, curators, and other art professionals. It includes many helpful links.

The History of Art Virtual Library

www.chart.ac.uk/vlib/   This site provides a wide range of links and images.

Art Source

www.ilpi.com/artsource/welcome.html   A selective but very useful site maintained by Mary Molinar of the University of Kentucky.

Image Collections and Online Art

www.umich.edu/%7Ehartspc/histart/mother/images.html Possibly the most comprehensive and helpful of all the online compendia of images and information about art history, this site has been developed at the University of Michigan.

Some Respected Journals

Art and Australia   This broadly based magazine is the leading Australian publication on the visual arts.

Art in America   A broad-ranging monthly magazine, aimed at the general public and art dealers as well as art historians.

Art History   This respected scholarly journal, published by the Association of Art Historians in the UK, is issued quarterly.

Art Journal   This scholarly journal, founded in 1941, is the flagship publication of the College Art Association.

Artforum   This monthly magazine provides good coverage of much of the contemporary art world.

Canadian Art   This broadly based magazine is the leading Canadian publication on the visual arts.

39c. BIOLOGY

Citation and Documentation

The Council of Science Editors (CSE) style is followed universally in biology. See the section elsewhere in this book on Citation and Documentation Systems for a full outline of CSE style.

Some Useful Websites

Agricola

www.agricola.nal.usda.gov   Provides a wide variety of materials relating to agriculture, animal science, and forestry.

Biology Online

www.biology-online.org   A wide-ranging source of information, with links to hundreds of other sites.

Canada Institute for Scientific and Technical Information

www.cisti-icist.nrc-cnrc.gc.ca   The collection includes technical reports and conference papers as well as journal articles.

Harvard BioLinks

www.mcb.harvard.edu/BioLinks.html   This site is posted by Harvard University's Department of Molecular and Cell Biology; it provides quick links to many key sources of information.

Pubmed Central

www.pubmedcentral.nih.gov   The US National Institutes of Health (NIH) free digital archive of biomedical and lifesciences journal literature.

Union of Concerned Scientists

www.ucsusa.org   This site provides a wide range of information regarding environmental problems and solutions.

Virtual Library: Biosciences

www.vlb.org/Biosciences   This section of the Virtual Library includes a wide range of useful information and links.

Some Respected Journals

Journal of Biological Chemistry   Founded in 1905, this journal covers new developments in many areas of biochemistry.

Journal of Cell Biology   Published every two weeks, this journal presents a wide range of new research in the field.

Journal of Bacteriology   Published every two weeks; a leading journal for reporting research on genetics and molecular biology as well as on bacteria.

Nature   Founded in 1869, this is one of the world's most prestigious scientific journals.

Quarterly Review of Biology   Founded in 1923, this journal includes reviews of books and software as well as review articles; aimed at the discipline as a whole.

39d. BUSINESS AND COMMERCE

Citation and Documentation

Although there is no universally accepted style of citation and documentation for business and commerce, APA Style is very widely used. See the section above on Citation and Documentation Systems for a full outline of APA style.

Some Useful Websites

Business.gov

www.business.gov   This US government site provides a wide range of statistics on business activity.

Global Edge

www.globaledge.msu.edu/ibrd/ibrd.asp   Provides a useful collection of information on international business.

JSTOR

www.jstor.org   Founded in 1995 as a not-for-profit organization, this site is a leader in providing electronic access to a wide variety of scholarly journals online.

Virtual Library: Business and Economics

www.vlib.org/BusinessEconomics   The business and economics section of the Virtual Library provides a wide variety of information and links.

Some Respected Journals

The Academy of Management Journal   This journal is respected for cutting-edge research.

Business Week   Founded in 1929, this popular weekly magazine provides accessible news and analysis.

Fortune   Founded in 1930, this respected twice-weekly magazine focuses on business and the economy.

The Journal of Business   Founded in 1928, this journal is published by the University of Chicago; it is perhaps the most prestigious academic journal in the discipline.

The Journal of Finance   This widely-cited journal is the official publication of the American Finance Association.

39e. CHEMISTRY

Citation and Documentation

American Chemical Society. *American Chemical Society Style Guide: A Manual for Authors and Editors*. 3rd ed. Washington: American Chemical Society Publishing, 3/e 2006. A summary is available online at www.pubs.acs.org/books/references.shtml.

Some Useful Websites

Links for Chemists

www.liv.ac.uk/chemistry/Links/links.html   Run by the University of Liverpool Chemistry department, this site is the chemistry section of the Virtual Library.

American Chemical Society

www.chemistry.org   The website of the American Chemical Society includes a wide variety of information, as well as links to other sites.

Cheminfo

www.indiana.edu/~cheminfo   A good general site run out of the University of Indiana.

Some Respected Journals

Chemical Reviews   Founded in 1924, this journal publishes review articles on all areas of the discipline.

American Chemical Society Journal   Founded in 1879, this journal is now published every two weeks; it is a key source for recent studies in all areas of the discipline.

Chemical Abstracts   Founded in 1907, this journal is unrivaled for comprehensiveness in presenting abstracts of chemistry articles.

39f. ECONOMICS

Citation and Documentation Style

Although there is no universally accepted style of documentation for economics, APA (American Psychological Association) style is very widely used. See the section elsewhere in this book on Citation and Documentation Systems for a full outline of APA style.

Some Useful Websites

History of Economic Thought

www.cepa.newschool.edu/net   This site provides a range of reliable summaries of key ideas and movements in the history of economics.

EconLit

www.econlit.org   This site, run through the American Economic Association, contains abstracts, indexes, and links to articles in most major economic journals. It is available at libraries and on university websites throughout the world.

WebEc

www.helsinki.fi/webec   WebEc worldwide Web resources in economics provides links to a vast amount of free information in economics.

Some Respected Journals

American Economic Review   Founded in 1911, this is the flagship journal of the American Economic Association.

Econometrica   An international journal of mathematical economics founded in 1933.

Economic Journal   This British journal was founded in 1891 and remains influential.

Journal of Economic Literature   This journal was created in 1969 by the American Economic Association in order to provide an annotated bibliography of publications in the discipline. It offers summaries of books and journal articles, and useful surveys of recent publications on particular topics within economics.

Journal of Economic History Founded in 1941, this journal has maintained a high reputation.

Journal of Political Economy   Founded in 1892 at the University of Chicago, this journal has in the past generation been a leading venue for the expression of neoclassical and monetarist views.

39g. ENGLISH STUDIES

Citation and Documentation

MLA style is standard in the discipline. See the section elsewhere in this book on Citation and Documentation Systems for a full outline of MLA style. For more on writing about literature see also pages 15–18 above.

Some Useful Websites

JSTOR

www.jstor.org   Founded in 1995 as a not-for-profit organization, this site is a leader in providing electronic access to a wide variety of scholarly journals online.

Literary Resources on the Net

www.andromeda.rutgers.edu/~lynch/Lit   Maintained by Jack Lynch of Rutgers University, this site provides access to a wide variety of reliable information.

Project Muse

www.muse.jhu.edu   This site, founded in 1995 by the Johns Hopkins University Press, provides access to a wide range of scholarly journals, with a strong emphasis on literature and culture.

Project Gutenberg

www.gutenberg.org   This site provides an extraordinarily wide-ranging collection of online texts in the public domain. Not all are reliably transcribed, but the site is nevertheless an invaluable resource.

Representative Poetry Online

www.eir.library.utoronto.ca/rpo/display/index.cfm   Run out of the University of Toronto, this site provides reliable texts and excellent notes for many English poems.

Some Respected Journals

American Literature   Founded in 1929, this journal is the most established of those specializing in American literature.

Canadian Literature   Founded in 1960, this journal is the leader among academic publications specializing in Canadian literature.

PMLA   Founded in 1844, this is the flagship journal of the Modern Languages Association (the leading association in North America for academics specializing in English Studies).

Review of English Studies   Published by Oxford University Press, this leading journal emphasizes historical scholarship rather than interpretive criticism.

Studies in English Literature   Published by Johns Hopkins University Press, this leading journal focuses on four fields of British Literature: English Renaissance, Tudor and Stuart Drama, Restoration and Eighteenth Century, and Nineteenth Century.

39h. HISTORY

Citation and Documentation

There is no universally accepted style of documentation for history. Many journals use some variety of Chicago Style; many use traditional footnotes or endnotes. For students the most important guideline is thus to follow whatever instructions each instructor may give you.

Some Useful Websites

Historical Journals Online

www2.tntech.edu/history/journals.html   Provides links to a wide variety of historical journals.

JSTOR

www.jstor.org   Founded in 1995 as a not-for-profit organization, this site is a leader in providing electronic access to a wide variety of scholarly journals online.

Labyrinth

www.georgetown.edu/labyrinth   This site provides access to a very wide range of materials on medieval history, including many primary sources.

Project Muse

www.muse.jhu.edu   This site, founded in 1995 by the Johns Hopkins University Press, provides access to a wide range of scholarly journals. The strongest emphasis is on literature and culture, but many historical journals are included as well.

Virtual Library: History

www.vlib.org/History   In this subject as in others, the Virtual Library provides access to a great deal of useful information.

Some Respected Journals

American Historical Review   Founded in 1895, this is the flagship journal of the American Historical Association; it covers all historical fields, not just American history.

Canadian Historical Review   Run by the Canadian Historical Association, this is the leading journal for articles on Canadian history.

English Historical Review   Founded in 1886, this journal is the oldest journal of historical scholarship in the English-speaking world, and it remains one of the most prestigious. Published by Oxford University Press, the journal covers world as well as British history.

History and Theory   Founded in 1960, this leading journal often features interdisciplinary articles.

39i. PHILOSOPHY

Citation and Documentation

There is no universally accepted style of documentation for philosophy. Many journals use some variety of Chicago Style; many use traditional footnotes or endnotes. For students the most important guideline is thus to follow whatever instructions each instructor may give you.

Some Useful Websites

JSTOR

www.jstor.org   Founded in 1995 as a not-for-profit organization, this site is a leader in providing electronic access to a wide variety of scholarly journals.

Philosophy Pages

www.philosophypages.com   A wide range of useful basic information in accessible form.

Project Muse

www.muse.jhu.edu   This site, founded in 1995 by the Johns Hopkins University Press, provides access to a wide range of scholarly journals, with a strong emphasis on literature and culture, but a good representation of philosophy journals as well.

Virtual Library: Philosophy

www.vlib.org   Click on Humanities and go to Philosophy. This section of the Virtual Library site is run through the University of Bristol.

Some Respected Journals

Australian Journal of Philosophy   A respected general journal.

Canadian Journal of Philosophy   A respected general journal.

Ethics   One of the leading journals for analytic articles on topics in ethics.

Journal of Philosophy   The most prestigious general journal in the discipline.

Mind   One of the leading journals for analytic articles on topics in the philosophy of mind.

Philosophy and Public Affairs   This respected journal is aimed at the general reader as well as an academic audience.

39j. PHYSICS

Citation and Documentation

American Institute of Physics. *Style Manual for Guidance in the Preparation of Papers.* 4th ed. New York: American Inst. of Physics, 1990–97.

Some Useful Websites

Net Advance of Physics

web.mit.edu/~redingtn/www/netadv/97welcome.html
This site, supported by MIT, offers a wide range of
information in an encyclopedic format.

Physics News

www.het.brown.edu/news/index.html   This site provides
information and links on all aspects of the subject.

Physics Today Online

www.physicstoday.org   This site, run by the American
Institute of Physics, offers information on recent research
and provides links to databases, societies, and a variety
of electronic publications.

Some Respected Journals

Annals of Physics   Publishes review articles intended to
be accessible to a broad audience.

Physical Review   The most established journal in the
discipline is divided into five sections on different
subdisciplines.

Physics Letters   This respected journal is divided into two
sections—Part A on General, Atomic, and Solid Physics,
and Part B on Nuclear, Elementary Particle, and High
Energy Physics.

39k. POLITICAL SCIENCE

Citation and Documentation

There is no universally accepted citation and
documentation system in this discipline, but the *Chicago
Manual of Style* is probably the most widely used.

Some Useful Websites

Canadian Supreme Court Decisions

www.lexum.umontreal.ca/csc-scc/en   Canadian Supreme
Court decisions may be accessed through this site.

Election Resources

www.electionresources.org   This site provides a wealth
of information on election results from nations around
the world.

JSTOR

www.jstor.org   Founded in 1995 as a not-for-profit
organization, this site is a leader in providing electronic
access to a wide variety of scholarly journals.

Virtual Library: International Affairs

www.vlib.org/internationalaffairs   A wide range of
useful information and links.

US Supreme Court

www.supremecourtus.gov   US Supreme Court opinions
may be accessed through the site.

Some Respected Journals

Canadian Journal of Political Science   The most
respected political science journal in Canada.

Congressional Quarterly   Focuses on American national
politics.

The Economist   The world's most authoritative weekly
news magazine.

Foreign Affairs   This quarterly journal publishes a wide
range of articles on international affairs. Aimed at the
general reader as well as the scholar.

Political Science Quarterly   Founded in 1886, this journal remains one of the most respected.

Washington Monthly A magazine that appeals to the general public as well as to scholars.

391. PSYCHOLOGY

Citation and Documentation
Virtually all academic writing in psychology follows the principles set out in the APA Style manual.

Some Useful Websites
American Psychological Association

www.apa.org   The APA site provides access to a wide range of useful information.

Classics in the History of Psychology

http://psychclassics.yorku.ca/   A useful archive of many key texts in the history of psychology.

Encyclopedia of Psychology

www.psychology.org   A helpful and wide-ranging site.

PsychWeb

www.psycwww.com   An informal site with a range of useful links.

Social Psychology Network

www.socialpsychology.org   Including a wide range of useful information, this site bills itself as "the largest social psychology database on the Internet."

Some Respected Journals
American Journal of Psychology   A leader in the discipline.

American Psychologist   A broad ranging monthly journal, founded in 1946.

Psychological Review   A quarterly journal with an emphasis on psychology theory, founded in 1894.

Journal of Personality and Social Psychology   Founded in 1965, this is the leading journal in the subdiscipline of social psychology.

39m. SOCIOLOGY

Citation and Documentation

The most widely accepted style of citation and documentation is that of the American Sociological Association (ASA Style). This is in many ways similar to other styles of parenthetical citation. Note, however, that page numbers may be given in the citation, and that in that case they are preceded by a colon:

> What Wright terms "idealized capitalism" (2000: 959) relates to the neoclassical economic model.

References are provided at the end of an essay, alphabetically by author:

> Pakulski, Jan and Malcolm Waters. 1996. *The Death of Class*. London: Sage.
> Wright, Erik Olin. 2000. "Working-class power, capitalist class interests, and class compromise." *American Journal of Sociology* 105: 957-1002.

Some Useful Websites

Auraria Library

www.library.auraria.edu   Established as a shared library for three universities in Denver, Colorado, the Auraria Library includes useful subject guides that provide access to a wealth of information.

American Sociological Association

www.asanet.org   This site provides a wide range of information about the discipline, together with useful links to other sites.

JSTOR

www.jstor.org   Founded in 1995 as a not-for-profit organization, this site is a leader in providing electronic access to a wide variety of scholarly journals.

Some Respected Journals

American Journal of Sociology   This highly-respected journal is published by the University of Chicago Press; it was founded 1895. Issues from recent years are available online at www.journals.uchicago.edu.

American Sociological Review   This wide-ranging and prestigious journal is published six times yearly; it is the flagship journal of the American Sociological Association. Available online through JSTOR.

Canadian Journal of Sociology   Published by the University of Toronto Press, this is the most highly respected of Canadian journals in the discipline.

Criminology   Probably the most highly respected journal in this important branch of sociology.

Social Forces   An influential interdisciplinary journal published by the University of North Carolina Press (also available through JSTOR).

Sociology   The flagship journal of the British Sociological Association.

Journal of Marriage and the Family   The leading North American journal in the area of the sociology of the family.

WRITING
BY COMPUTER

40. COMPUTERS AND THE WRITING PROCESS

40a. WHAT COMPUTERS CAN AND CAN'T DO

No one born later than, say, 1950, needs to be convinced of the advantages of computers for writing. But many of us need to remind ourselves periodically of some of the pitfalls of word-processed writing. Some problems are readily avoided if one retains the habit of careful proofreading: the perils of spell-check, for example (see below) or the dangers of search and replace. It is all too easy to come to rely on the computer a little too heavily in such contexts—as I found myself doing recently when I instructed my computer to do a search and replace on a contract, replacing all occurrences of "author" in the contract with the words "senior editor." What need could there be to confirm? The contract was almost in the mail before "senior editorization" and "senior editority" caught my eye. I certainly had not *senior editor*ized the change, but my computer had no way of stopping once I had unleashed its search and replace engine.

Proofreading may check some of the bad cognitive habits that computers breed in many writers who work only on screen; it certainly will not eliminate them all. For some of us, computers can be wonderful facilitators of flow; many people find it easier to get a lot of ideas out of their heads and "on paper" by using a computer than by using a pen and paper. But the same habits of scrolling that can facilitate flow in writing and in reading can distort our ability to arrange ideas in an ordered fashion so as to best present an argument. Though researchers are far from understanding why, they have assembled a considerable body of evidence suggesting that seeing a succession of printed pages enables one to combine and connect ideas in ways that are not always evident if one restricts oneself to scrolling on the screen. This is why it is vitally important to work with paper as well as on screen. It is ironic that the very means by which the reordering of blocks of text has become a matter of effortlessly keyboarding (rather than of cutting, pasting, and retyping) also acts to dull the cognitive processes that are required for humans to re-order those blocks most effectively. But that is the reality all writers must come to terms with.

If computer technology may facilitate the sort of writing flow that is the best tonic for writer's block, the speed with which that technology changes may also sometimes give us an excuse not to write. It is all too easy to decide that it will be impossible to finish a thesis or complete a report unless and until one upgrades software, replaces that old hard drive, or acquires a faster machine. In almost all cases this is really just a way of trying to avoid the hard job of getting down to writing. We should all make it a firm rule not to let our fascination with technology get in the way of our writing.

40b. A NOTE ON SPELL-CHECK

Commonly used words are also commonly misspelled words—and not only because they occur frequently. Most of us have the sense when we use a word such as *surreptitiously* to check the spelling in a dictionary, or with the spell-check mechanism on our computer. But words such as *its* and *it's*, or *than* and *then*, or *compliment* and *complement* we tend to use without thinking—and no computer spell-check will tell us if we have had a mental lapse and used the wrong one. It is worth remembering that no computer can be a substitute for careful proofreading.

It is always a good idea to run your work through a grammar checker before submitting it. Though MS Word's grammar checker is free, the Editor program from Serenity Software is in many ways superior.

40c. THE INTERNET

In 1992 the media was full of references to the need to create an "electronic highway." But within a year almost everyone had realised that one had already been created. The Internet had originally been the product of the American Defence Department's desire to build diffuse lines of communication as a defense against attacks on the country's infrastructure. Made available for use by academics in the 1980s, it had quietly developed by the early 1990s into an extraordinarily efficient and inexpensive means of communication. And as Web technology has developed, its potential has continued to grow. Technology that can be used in so many ways can of course also be misused in many ways. Given the pace of change—and the complexity of the topic—it would be unwise in a book of this size to attempt any comprehensive treatment of how to use the Internet as a resource tool for writing. But some general guidelines may be useful.

40d. RESEARCH USING THE INTERNET

The Internet may seem like a gold mine when it comes to research. But if so, the likeness is to a vein of ore that is not always sufficiently concentrated as to make the mining of it economic. Sometimes the most difficult thing is to decide when it is worth one's while to commit one's resources to the mining operation. Search engines are likely to turn up vast amounts of material on almost any topic. But often much of it will be unreliable—and it is extraordinarily difficult for the novice to tell what is likely to be reliable and what isn't.

At one end of the spectrum, most refereed scholarly journals are available online—and some are available *only* on the Internet. The best way to consult reference works that are constantly updated (such as the *Oxford English Dictionary*) is through the Internet. And, some academic disciplines are now turning to publication via the Internet for new scholarly monographs.

At the other end of the spectrum are countless materials that have not been reviewed either by academic authorities or by publishers. How is one to gauge the reliability of such material? Should one just stick to established sources in the library? How is it possible to avoid spending a large amount of time merely to amass a large quantity of unreliable source material?

There are no easy answers to these questions, and the best strategies are likely to vary depending on the sort of research one is doing. The most important thing for the novice may be simply to consult one's instructor on the issue of what sources —whether in the library or on the Internet—may be most appropriate to use for a given assignment.

Some other research principles may be helpful. Think of the credentials of the author; is he or she an academic at a respected institution, and has he or she published widely on the topic? How new is the material? (Obviously some premium is to be placed on more recent research, though often the most important works on a topic will not be new.) Which works on a topic are cited most often by others? If a work is frequently cited by others, it will be one that should be taken into account. What is the point of view of the author? One key consideration in assembling the resources one will deal with is making sure that a variety of viewpoints are represented.

You should not feel obliged, though, to give equal weight to all points of view. Particularly where material on the Web is concerned, it will sometimes be the case that implausible or downright irresponsible points of view will be more widely represented than views that deserve greater respect. Such is obviously the case with websites promulgating racist or anti-Semitic views, but it may also be the case with certain scientific matters. By the late 1990s, for example, the vast majority of reputable scientific opinion was in broad agreement as to the dangers of global warming. Dissenting scientific voices comprised only a small minority among the community of reputable scientists—but for years their views received disproportionate space on the Web, where numerous sites were largely devoted to casting doubt on the consensus scientific view on global warming (and, not by coincidence, to preserving the status quo for the coal industry, the oil and gas industry, and so on). Where such ideologically charged issues as these are concerned, it is worth paying particularly close attention to accounts that run counter to the normal ideological stance of the publication. When the right-wing magazine *The Economist* accepted several years ago that the weight of evidence overwhelmingly supported the argument that global warming posed a real danger, or when the left-of-centre British newspaper *The Guardian* concluded that despite its socialist rhetoric the Mugabe government in Zimbabwe was denying its people both economic justice and basic human rights, such views deserve special respect.

With library sources, the publisher of a work is also a helpful clue for the researcher. The experienced researcher will take account of the publisher, but not put too much stock in its reputation; the university presses of Oxford, Cambridge, Harvard, and Princeton have published a few real clunkers as well as vast amounts of first-rate scholarship. And, because librarians often have standing orders from such prestigious presses as these, a clunker from them is more likely to find its way onto the shelves of the university library than a clunker from, say, Wilfrid Laurier Press or from Hackett Publishing. Nevertheless, there will always be a better than average chance of work published by a highly reputable organization being of high quality. This holds true for the Web as well. The beginning student will often not know which journals or which book publishers have a solid track record. But it will help to be wary of self-published material, whether in book form or on the Web, and it will help as well if the researcher pays attention to such matters, and is prepared to ask questions of instructors and of fellow students.

Perhaps above all, it is important to note each source you consult in writing an essay, report, or thesis. (Be sure as well to mark clearly any passages or phrases that are a direct quotation rather than a summary or your own commentary on what you have read, so as not to confuse your own ideas or phrasings with those of the authors you have consulted.) In the case of an Internet reference it may be more convenient to store the information on your hard drive or on a flash drive rather than on a card or piece of paper—but the principle of noting sources carefully remains the same.

If many of the principles are the same, the mechanisms of Web research are very different from the mechanisms of using the library, and are constantly changing. A number of good guidebooks devoted entirely to using Internet sources are now available,* and are updated regularly. Referencing styles also change frequently. Some of the essential points of referencing Internet sources appear above in the section on documentation.

*See for example Andrew Harnack and Eugene Kleppinger's *Online: A Reference Guide to Using Internet Sources* (New York: St. Martin's).

40e. OBSERVING NETIQUETTE

"Netiquette" is a clever little pun that neatly encapsulates the notion that standards of courtesy and consideration are as important in cyberspace as they are in other areas of human existence—and that the Internet is sufficiently different from other forms of communication as to make some special guidelines advisable.

Anyone who has used email has probably sensed that the medium lends itself to a higher degree of informality (for both sender and recipient) than does the sending of a letter printed on corporate or departmental letterhead. The combination of distance, informality, and invisibility that electronic communication embodies seems to encourage the spontaneous expression of emotion in ways that might otherwise not feel appropriate. It often seems to foster a breeziness that is as friendly as it is efficient. But it also seems to lend itself to the venting of certain sorts of anger, in ways that other means of communication do not. And sometimes it leads people to divulge personal information that on reflection they might rather have kept to themselves. These tendencies of email—to foster sometimes unexpected degrees of intimacy, and to facilitate the unbridled expression of anger—argue for the wisdom of taking the time to edit and proof any electronic message, checking its tone quite as much as its grammar.

The ever-increasing use of electronic communication in a wide variety of contexts continues to raise issues of appropriate tone and of level of formality. For the most part, no one expects emails to conform to all the conventions of more formal communications; it would be foolish to worry about a typo or two in an email dashed off to a friend—let alone a text message! But any email should be clear, unambiguous, and written in an appropriate tone; again, it is wise to edit and proofread carefully any message you send. And, if you are using email as a convenient way to convey a more formal document, that document should indeed conform to the conventions of standard usage. A proposal submitted electronically or a memo circulated electronically should be phrased, proofed, and presented as carefully as you would the same document in hard copy form. As with writing, faxing, or phoning, then, the context and the expectations of your audience are always important.

Privacy issues are at least as important with electronic communications as they are with other forms of communication. As a recipient, consider the feelings of the sender; unless it is obviously appropriate to forward a message, for example, ask the permission of the sender before you pass it on.

Senders should remember that electronic communication can often end up being less private than regular mail. Recipients are not always as considerate as one might wish. And, particularly given that emails are often forwarded or copied by mistake to unintended recipients, it is wise to consider whether the potential recipients of a message may be a much larger group than intended—and to word the message accordingly.

40f. POINT-FORM NETIQUETTE

- Keep messages clear and brief.
- Edit/proof all messages before sending—for tone as well as form.
- Use clear subject headings.
- Make the text as easy to read as possible; leave a line between paragraphs (rather than indenting); for italics place an underscore mark before and after the relevant word(s); use only well-known abbreviations.
- When quoting from a previous message, quote only the necessary passage(s).
- Address the message carefully.
- Attachments: if you want to send an attachment to a message, check first with the recipient if it will be possible to download. The alternative (provided the material is no more than a few pages long) is to embed material from another document into your message.
- Visuals: remember that your recipient may not have the same technology you do. Think twice, for example, before sending a large file of graphic information that may take the recipient an inordinate amount of time to download, if indeed (s)he has the capacity to do so.
- Listservs/chatgroups/newsgroups/bulletin boards: There are a variety of Internet mechanisms for sharing information among many individuals with

a common interest. Conventions may vary with each group; it makes sense to pay attention to the procedures followed and the tone adopted by established users before you start to play an active role yourself. If in any doubt as to appropriate procedures, ask the listowner/bulletin board organizer.

- Post only information that is likely to be of interest to others—and, as with email, be as clear and as brief as possible.

- Be particularly sensitive to the demands you may be making on the time of others. If, for example, you are sending an 'information-only' email to a department head who may deal with a hundred emails a day, make it clear in the heading or at the beginning of the message that this is for information only, and that no reply is required.

- The overriding principle: always show consideration for your reader(s).

40g. PLAGIARISM, COPYRIGHT, AND THE WEB

(See also pages 90–91.)

Keeping careful track of your sources—and clearly indicating for your own reference what is a quotation and what is your own comment on a work you have consulted—not only saves time; it also prevents unintentional plagiarism.

Although the possibilities both for unintended and for intentional plagiarism are vastly greater with the Web than they were when hard copy materials were the only resources, the mechanisms for detection have expanded as well; search engines can often confirm for an instructor in seconds that a particular string of words in a student essay has been lifted unacknowledged from another source.

Copyright rules for written materials apply to the Internet just as they do to books or articles; written work is under copyright protection for many years after it is published.* Except for quoting brief passages (with the proper acknowledgement), you may not reproduce material from the Web without the permission of the copyright holder. Nor may you post copyrighted materials on the Web without permission from the copyright holders.

*In the United States the 1998 Sonny Bono Copyright Amendment Act significantly extended copyright protection; most written material published in 1924 or later will remain in copyright for many years to come; in the UK and other European countries work is in copyright for seventy years after the death of the author (or translator); in Canada work is in copyright for fifty years after the death of the author or translator.

GLOSSARY OF USAGE

accept/except: *Accept* is a verb meaning to receive something favourably; *except* is a conjunction meaning *not including* or *but*. ("All the members of the Security Council except China voted to accept the proposal.")

advice/advise: *Advice* is the noun, *advise* is the verb. ("We advised them to proceed, but they did not take our advice.")

affect/effect: *Effect* is normally used as a noun meaning result. *Affect* is a verb meaning *cause* a result. ("There is no visible effect; perhaps nothing we can do will affect it.") Note, however, that *effect* may also be used as a verb meaning *put into effect*, as in "The changes were effected by the committee."

a lot: Two words.

all right: Two words.

allusion: See *illusion*.

already, all ready: When used as an adverb, *already* is one word. ("They were all ready to do the job, but he had already done it.")

altogether, all together: One word when used as an adverb to mean *completely* or *entirely*. ("He is not altogether happy with the result." "They were all together for the picnic.")

anyone: One word unless it is followed by *of*.

anyways/anywheres: There is never a need for the *s*.

assure/ensure/insure: To *assure* someone of something is to tell them with confidence or certainty; to *insure* (or *ensure*) that something will happen is to make sure that it does; to *insure* something is to purchase insurance on it so as to protect yourself in case of loss.

beg the question: To *beg the question* is to take for granted the very thing to be argued about. In recent years the phrase has been widely used to mean *invite the question*.

can/may: *Can* is used to refer to ability, *may* to refer to permission. ("He asked if he might leave the room.")

capital/capitol: *Capitol* refers to an American legislative building or a Roman temple; *capital* can refer to wealth, to the city from which a government operates, or to the top of a pillar; it may also be used as an adjective to mean *most important* or *principal*.

change: You <u>make</u> a *change* (not *do* a change).

childish/childlike: The first is a term of censure, the second a term of praise.

classic/classical: As adjectives, *classic* means of such high quality that it has lasted or will last for a long time, and *classical* means *pertaining to ancient Greece and Rome* or, particularly when speaking of music, *written in a traditional style*. ("Sophocles was a great classical author; his plays are acknowledged classics.")

climatic/climactic: Weather is not the most exciting part. ("Climatic projections concerning average temperature are often inaccurate." "He spilled his drink at the most climactic moment in the movie.")

compliment/complement: To *compliment* people is to praise them, and a *compliment* is the praise; to *complement* something is to add to it to make it better or complete, and a *complement* is the number or amount needed to make it complete. ("None of the divisions had its full complement of troops, and the troops were complimented on the good job they had done despite being short-staffed.")

comprise/compose: The whole *comprises* or includes the various parts; the parts *compose* the whole.

conscience/conscious/consciousness: To be *conscious* is to be awake and aware of what is happening, whereas *conscience* is a part of our minds that tells us what is right or wrong to do. ("Her conscience told her not to steal the chocolate bar.")

continual/continuous: If something is *continuous* it never stops; something *continual* is frequently repeated but not unceasing. ("He has been phoning me continually for the past two weeks.")

could of: A corruption of *could have*.

council/counsel; **councillor/counsellor**: A *council* is a group of officials, and a *councillor* is a member of that group. *Counsel* is advice or, in the special case of a lawyer, the person offering advice. In other situations the person offering *counsel* is a *counsellor*.

definite/definitive: If something is *definite* then there is no uncertainty about it; a *definitive* version of something fixes it in its final or permanent form.

deny/refute: To *deny* something is to assert that it is not true; to *refute* it is to prove conclusively that it is not true. ("After weeks of denying the allegations he was finally able to produce evidence to refute them.")

discrete/discreet: *Discrete* means separate or distinct, whereas *discreet* means prudent and tactful; unwilling to give away secrets. ("The Queen is renowned for being discreet.")

disinterested/uninterested: A *disinterested* person is unbiased; uninfluenced by self-interest, especially of a monetary sort. If one is *uninterested* in something, one is bored by it.

effect: See *affect*.

elicit/illicit: *Elicit* is a verb; one elicits information about something. *Illicit* is an adjective meaning illegal or not approved.

emigrate/immigrate: To *emigrate* is to leave a country; to *immigrate* is to move to it. ("More than 10,000 emigrants from the United States became immigrants to Canada last year.")

enthuse/enthusiastic: *Enthuse* is a verb; *enthused* is its past participle. The adjective is *enthusiastic*. ("Everyone was enthusiastic about the movie.")

everyday/every day: One word when used as an adjective to mean "daily," but two words when used to mean "each day." ("Brushing your teeth should be part of your everyday routine." "She comes here every day.")

everyone: One word unless it is followed by *of*.

explicit/implicit: Something *explicit* is stated in precise terms, not merely suggested or implied. By contrast, something *implicit* is not stated overtly.

farther/further: *Farther* refers to physical distance, *further* to time or degree. ("We do not have much farther to go." "The plan needed further study.")

flaunt/flout: To *flout* is to disobey or show disrespect for; to *flaunt* is to display very openly. ("The demonstrators openly flouted the law.")

forget: To *forget* something is to fail to remember it, not to leave it somewhere. ("I left my book at home" or "I forgot to bring my book" but not "I forgot my book at home.")

forward/foreword: You find a *foreword* before the other words in a book.

good/well: The most common of the adjective-for-adverb mistakes. ("He pitched very well today.") See page 50.

hardly: *Hardly* acts as a negative; there is thus no need to add a second negative. ("They claim that you can hardly tell the difference.")

historic/historical: *Historic* means *of sufficient importance that it is likely to become famous in history* (a historic occasion). *Historical* means *having to do with history* (historical research).

hopefully: Traditionalists argue that the correct meaning of the adverb *hopefully* is *filled with hope*, and that the use of the word to mean *it is to be hoped that* is therefore incorrect. Others argue, plausibly, that many other adverbs may function as independent comments at the beginning of a sentence ("Finally, ..." "Clearly, ..." "Obviously, ...") and that there is no good reason for treating *hopefully* differently. Using *hopefully* to mean *it is to be hoped that* should not be regarded as a grievous error—but it is a form of English usage that will upset many instructors.

infer/imply: To *imply* something is to suggest it without stating it directly; the other person will have to *infer* your meaning. ("This sentence implies that the character is not to be trusted.")

illusion/allusion: An *allusion* is an indirect reference to something; an *illusion* is something falsely supposed to exist. ("Her poem makes many allusions to Shakespeare.") Also, when you make an *allusion*, you are alluding to something.

increase: Numbers can be *increased* or *decreased*, as can such things as production and population (nouns which refer to certain types of numbers or quantities). Things such as *houses*, however, or *books* (nouns which do not refer to numbers or quantities) cannot be *increased*; only the number of houses, books, etc. can be *increased* or *decreased*, *raised* or *lowered*.

irregardless/regardless: There is no need for the extra syllable; use *regardless*.

is when/is where: Avoid these expressions when defining something. ("Osmosis occurs when...," not "Osmosis is when....")

its/it's: *Its* is an adjective meaning *belonging to it*. *It's* is a contraction of *it is*—a pronoun plus a verb. ("It's true that a coniferous tree continually sheds its leaves.")

later/latter: *Later* means afterwards in time, whereas the *latter* is the last mentioned of two things.

lay/lie: You *lay* something on the table, and a hen *lays* eggs, but you *lie* down to sleep. In other words, *lie* is an intransitive verb; it should not be followed by a direct object. *Lay*, by contrast, is transitive. ("That old thing has been lying around for years.")

lend/loan: In formal English *loan* should be used only as a noun; *lend* is the verb. ("He was unwilling to lend his sister any money.")

less/fewer: Use *less* only with uncountable nouns; use *fewer* with anything that can be counted. ("This checkout is for people buying fewer than twelve items.")

liable/likely: Do not use *liable* unless you are referring to possible undesirable consequences. ("It is liable to explode at any moment.")

like/as: In formal writing use the conjunction *as* to introduce a clause—not the preposition *like*. ("He looks like his father." "He looks as his father did at his age.")

literally: A literal meaning is the opposite of a figurative or metaphorical meaning. Do not use *literally* simply to emphasize what you are saying.

loose/lose: *Loose* is normally used as an adjective meaning *not tight*; *lose* is always a verb. ("The rope has come loose." "He began to lose control of himself.")

may be/maybe: One word when used as an adverb to mean "possibly," but two words when used as a verb. ("Maybe he will arrive later tonight." "He may be here later tonight.")

may of: A corruption of *may have*.

might of: A corruption of *might have*.

mitigate/militate: To *mitigate* something is to make it less harsh or severe ("mitigating circumstances"); to *militate* against something is to act as a strong influence against it.

must of: A corruption of *must have*.

nor: Use in combination with *neither*, not in combination with *not*. When using *not* use *or* instead of *nor*. ("She does not drink or smoke." "She neither drinks nor smokes.")

nothing/nobody/nowhere: These words should not be used with another negative word such as *not*. With *not* use *anything*, *anybody*, *anywhere*. ("He could not do anything about it.")

per cent/percentage: If you use *per cent*, you must give the number. Otherwise use *percentage*. ("The percentage of people who responded was very small.")

persuade: If one does not succeed in making people believe or do what one wants, then one has not persuaded or convinced them, but only *tried* to persuade them.

precede/proceed: To *precede* is to come before; to *proceed* is to go forward. ("Once the students understood that *G* precedes *H* in the alphabet, they proceeded with the lesson.")

prescribe/proscribe: To *prescribe* something is to recommend or order its use; to *proscribe* something is to forbid its use.

principal/principle: *Principal* can be either a noun or an adjective. As a noun it means *the person in the highest position of authority in an organization* (e.g., a school principal) or *an amount of money*, as distinguished from the interest on it. As an adjective it means *first in rank or importance.* ("The principal city of northern Nigeria is Kano.") *Principle* is always a noun; a principle is *a basic truth or doctrine*, *a code of conduct*, or *a law describing how something works.* ("We feel this is a matter of principle.")

quote/quotation: *Quote* is the verb, *quotation* the noun. ("The following quotation illustrates the point.")

real/really: *Real* is the adjective, *really* the adverb. ("She was really happy.")

reason is because: Use *that* instead of *because* to avoid redundancy. ("The reason may have been that they were uncertain of the ally's intentions.")

respectively/respectfully: *Respectively* means *in the order mentioned*; *respectfully* means *done with respect.* ("Green Bay, Denver, and San Francisco are, respectively, the three best teams in the league.")

sensory/sensuous/sensual: Advertising and pornography have dulled the distinction among these three adjectives; *sensual* is the one relating to sexual pleasure.

set/sit: *Set* means *to place something somewhere.*

short/scarce: If people are *short* of something, that thing is *scarce.* ("Food is now extremely scarce throughout the country.")

since (1): As a time word, *since* is used to refer to the <u>point</u> at which a period of time began ("since six o'clock," "since 2008"). *For* is used to refer to the *amount* of time that has passed ("for two years," "for centuries"). ("He has been with us for three weeks" or "He has been with us since three weeks ago.")

since (2): Watch for ambiguity involving *since* meaning *because*, and *since* meaning *from the time that*; "Since he crashed his car he has been travelling very little" could mean either "Because he crashed his car..." or "From the time that he crashed his car...."

should of: A corruption of *should have*.

so: *So* should not be used in formal writing as an intensifier in the way that *very* is used. ("He looked very handsome," not "He looked so handsome.")

some/someone: With negatives (*not, never,* etc.) *any* is used in place of *some*. ("He never gives me any help.")

stationary/stationery: *Stationary* means *not moving; stationery* is what you write on. ("The cars were stationary.")

suppose/supposed: Be sure to add the *d* in the expression *supposed to*. ("We are supposed to be there now.")

sure and: In formal writing always use *sure to*, not *sure and*.

than/that: *Than* is the one used for comparative statements ("more than we had expected").

thankful/grateful: We are *thankful* that something has happened and *grateful* for something we have received. ("I am very grateful for the kind thoughts expressed in your letter.")

they/there/their/they're: Four words that are confused perhaps more frequently than any others. *They* is a pronoun used to replace any plural noun (e.g., books, people, numbers). *There* can be used to mean *in* (or *at*) *that place*, or can be used as an introductory word before various forms of the verb *to be* (*There is, There had been*, etc.). *Their* is a possessive adjective meaning *belonging to them*. Beware in particular of substituting *they* for *there*. ("There were many people in the crowd," *not* "They were many people in the crowd.")

tiring/tiresome: Something that is *tiring* makes you feel tired, though you may have enjoyed it very much. Something that is *tiresome* is tedious and unpleasant.

to/too/two: *Too* can mean *also* or be used to indicate excess (*too many, too heavy*); *two* is of course the number. ("She seemed to feel that there was too much to do.")

try and: In formal writing always use *try to*, not *try and*. ("He had agreed not to try to convert them.")

unexceptional/unexceptionable: *Unexceptional* means *ordinary, not an exception*; if something is *unexceptionable*, then you do not object (or *take exception*) to the thing in question.

unique/universal/perfect/complete/correct: None of these can be a matter of degree. Something is either unique or not unique, perfect or imperfect, and so on, never *very unique* or *quite perfect*.

use/used: Be sure to add the *d* in the expression *used to*. ("This neighbourhood used to be very different.")

valid/true/accurate: An *accurate* statement is one that is factually correct. A combination of *accurate* facts may not always give a *true* picture, however. *Valid* is often used carelessly and as a consequence may seem fuzzy in its meaning. Properly used it can mean *legally acceptable*, or *sound in reasoning*; do not use it to mean *accurate*, *reasonable*, *true*, or *well-founded*.

were/where: *Were* is of course a past tense form of the verb *to be*, while *where* refers to place.

whose/who's: *Whose* means *belonging to whom*; *who's* is a contraction of *who is*.

would of: A corruption of *would have*.

your/you're: *Your* shows possession, *you're* is a contraction of *you are*.

ON THE WEB

Exercises on words that may cause confusion and on other points of usage may be found at **www.broadviewpress.com/writing**. Click on **Exercises** and go to **B13–B207**.

A REFERENCE GUIDE TO BASIC GRAMMAR

PARTS OF SPEECH

NOUNS

Nouns are words that name people, things, places, or qualities. Some examples follow:

NAMES OF PEOPLE
boy
John
parent

NAMES OF THINGS
hat
spaghetti
fish

NAMES OF PLACES
Saskatoon
Zambia
New York

NAMES OF QUALITIES
silence
intelligence
anger

Nouns can be used to fill the gaps in sentences like these:

1) I saw_____at the market yesterday.
2) He dropped the _____into the gutter.
3) Has she lost a lot of _____?
4) Hamilton is a _____with several
5) hundred thousand _____living in it.

For a discussion of count and non-count nouns, see above, pages 55–56.

PRONOUNS

Pronouns replace or stand for nouns. For example, instead of saying, "The man slipped on a banana peel" or "George slipped on a banana peel," we can replace the noun *man* (or the noun *George*) with the pronoun *he* and say "He slipped on a banana peel."

Definite and Indefinite Pronouns: Whereas a pronoun such as *he* refers to a definite person, the words *each, every, either, neither, one, another,* and *much* are indefinite. They may be used as pronouns or as adjectives; for a discussion of issues involving these words see pages 27–29 and 47–49.

Each player wants to do his best.
(Here the word *each* is an adjective, describing the noun *player*.)

Each wants to do his best.
(Here the word *each* is a pronoun, acting as the subject of the sentence.)

Each of the players wants to do his best.
(The word *each* is still a pronoun, this time followed by the phrase *of the players*. But it is the pronoun *each* that is the subject of the sentence; the verb must be the singular *wants*.)

Possessive Pronouns and Adjectives:
See under *Adjectives* below.

Relative Pronouns: These pronouns relate back to a noun that has been used earlier in the same sentence. Look at how repetitious these sentences sound:

I talked to the man. The man wore a red hat.

We could of course replace the second *man* with *he*. Even better, though, is to relate or connect the second idea to the first by using a relative pronoun:

I talked to the man who wore a red hat.

I found the pencil. I had lost the pencil.
I found the pencil that I had lost.

The following are all relative pronouns:

who   whose (has other uses too)
which   that (has other uses too)
whom

Pronouns Acting as Subject and as Object:

For discussion of issues involving subject and object
pronouns see pages 48–49.

ARTICLES

These are words used to introduce nouns. There are only
three of them—*a, an,* and *the.* Articles show whether or
not one is drawing attention to a <u>particular</u> person or
thing. For discussion of issues involving the use of articles
see pages 54–56.

ADJECTIVES

Adjectives are words used to tell us more about (*describe*
or *modify*) nouns or pronouns. Here are some examples
of adjectives:

big   good   heavy
small   bad   expensive
pretty   careful   fat
quick   slow   thin

e.g. The fat man lifted the heavy table.

> (Here the adjective *fat* describes or tells us more about the noun
> *man,* and the adjective *heavy* describes the noun *table.*)

e.g. The fast runner finished ahead of the slow one.
> (*Fast* describes *runner,* and *slow* describes *one.*)

Notice that adjectives usually come before the nouns that they describe. This is not always the case, however; when the verb *to be* is used, adjectives often come after the noun or pronoun, and after the verb:

e.g. That woman is particularly careful about her finances.
> (*Careful* describes *woman.*)

e.g. It is too difficult for me to do.
> (*Difficult* describes *it.*)

Adjectives can be used to fill the gaps in sentences like these:

1) This _____ sweater was knitted by hand.
2) As soon as we entered the _____ house we heard a _____ clap of thunder.
3) Those shoes are very _____.
4) Derrida's argument at this point could fairly be described as _____.

Some words can be either adjectives or pronouns, depending on how they are used. That is the case with the indefinite pronouns (see above), and also with certain possessives (words that show possession):

POSSESSIVE ADJECTIVES

my	our
your	your
his/her	their
whose	whose

POSSESSIVE PRONOUNS

mine	ours
yours	yours
his/hers	theirs
whose	whose

e.g. I have my cup, and he has his.

> (Here the word *his* is a pronoun, used in place of the noun *cup*.)

e.g. He has his cup.

> (Here the word *his* is an adjective, describing the noun *cup*.)

e.g. Whose book is this?

> (Here the word *whose* is a possessive adjective, describing the *book*.)

e.g. Whose is this?

> (Here the word *whose* is a possessive pronoun, acting as the subject of the sentence.)

VERBS

Verbs are words that express actions or states of affairs. Most verbs can be conveniently thought of as *doing* words (e.g., *feel, do, carry, see, think, combine, send*) but a few verbs do not fit into this category. Indeed, the most common verb of all—*be*—expresses a state of affairs, not a particular action that is done.

Verbs are used to fill gaps in sentences like these:

1) I _____ very quickly, but I _____ not _____ up with my brother.
2) She usually _____ to sleep at 9:30.
3) Stephen _____ his breakfast very quickly.
4) They _____ a large farm near Newcastle.
5) There _____ many different languages that people in India _____.

One thing that makes verbs different from other parts of speech is that verbs have *tenses*; in other words, they change their form depending on the time you are talking about. For example, the present tense of the verb *to be* is *I am, you are, he is*, etc., while the past tense is *I was, you were, he was*, etc. If you are unsure whether or not a particular word is a verb, one way to check is to ask if it has different tenses. For example, if one thought that perhaps the word *football* might be a verb, one need only ask oneself if it would be correct to say, I *footballed*, I *am footballing*, I *will football*, and so on. Obviously it would not be, so one knows that *football* is the noun that names the game, not a verb that expresses an action. For a discussion of issues involving the use of verbs see pages 34–43.

ADVERBS

These words are usually used to tell us more about (*describe* or *modify*) verbs, although they can also be used to tell us more about adjectives or about other adverbs. They answer questions such as "How...?", "When...?", and "To what extent...?", and often they end with the letters *ly*. Here are a few examples, with the adjectives also listed for comparison.

ADJECTIVE	ADVERB
careful	carefully
beautiful	beautifully
thorough	thoroughly
sudden	suddenly
slow	slowly
easy	easily
good	well
	today
	often
	very

He walked carefully.
(The adverb *carefully* tells us <u>how</u> he walked; it describes the verb *walked*.)

He is a careful boy.
(The adjective *careful* describes the noun *boy*.)

My grandfather died suddenly last week.
(The adverb *suddenly* tells <u>how</u> he died; it describes the verb *died*.)

We were upset by the sudden death of my grandfather.

(The adjective *sudden* describes the noun *death*.)

She plays the game very well.

(The adverb *well* tells us <u>how</u> she plays; it describes the verb *plays*. The adverb *very* describes the adverb *well*.)

She played a good game this afternoon.

(The adjective *good* describes the noun *game*.)

She played a very good game.

(The adverb *very* describes the adjective *good*, telling us <u>how</u> good it was.)

According to his Press Secretary, Obama will meet Putin soon.

(The adverb *soon* describes the verb *will meet*, telling <u>when</u> the action will happen.)

Adverbs are used to fill gaps such as these:

1) Ralph writes very _____.
2) The Judge spoke _____ to Milken after he had been convicted on six counts of stock manipulation and fraud.
3) They were _____ late for the meeting this morning.

PREPOSITIONS

Prepositions are joining words, normally used before nouns or pronouns. Some of the most common prepositions are as follows:

after	from	off
across	in	over
at	into	to
before	of	until
for	on	with

Prepositions are used to fill gaps such as these:

1) I will tell you _____it _____the morning.
2) Please try to arrive _____eight o'clock.
3) He did not come back _____Toronto _____yesterday.
4) I received a letter _____my sister.

CONJUNCTIONS

Conjunctions are normally used to join groups of words together, and in particular to join clauses together. Some examples:

because	unless	after
although	until	if
and	since	or
as	before	that

They stopped playing because they were tired.

(The conjunction *because* joins the group of words "they were tired" to the group of words "they stopped playing.")

I will give her your message if I see her.

(The conjunction *if* introduces the second group of words and joins it to the first.)

Many conjunctions can also act as other parts of speech, depending on how they are used. Notice the difference in each of these pairs of sentences:

He will not do anything about it until the morning.

(Here *until* is a preposition joining the phrase *the morning* to the rest of the sentence.)

He will not do anything about it until he has discussed it with his wife.

(Here *until* is a conjunction introducing the clause "he has discussed it with his wife.")

I slept for half an hour after dinner.

(Here *after* is a preposition joining the noun *dinner* to
the rest of the sentence.)

I slept for half an hour after they had gone home.

(Here *after* is a conjunction introducing the clause "they
had gone home.")

She wants to buy that dress.

(Here *that* is an adjective describing the noun *dress*:
"Which dress?", "<u>That</u> dress!")

George said that he was unhappy.

(Here *that* is a conjunction introducing the clause
"he was unhappy.")

Conjunctions are used to fill gaps such as these:

1) We believed _____ we would win.
2) They sat down in the shade _____ it was hot.
3) My father did not speak to me _____ he left.

PARTS OF SENTENCES

SUBJECT

The subject is the thing, person, or quality about which
something is said in a clause. The subject is usually a
noun or pronoun.

The man went to town.

(The sentence is about the man, not about the town; thus the noun
man is the subject.)

Groundnuts are an important crop in Nigeria.

(The sentence is about groundnuts, not about crops or about
Nigeria; thus the noun *groundnut* is the subject.)

Nigeria is the most populous country in Africa.

(The sentence is about Nigeria, not about countries or about
Africa; thus the noun *Nigeria* is the subject.)

He followed me to the grocery store.

(The pronoun *He* is the subject.)

Core Subject (or "Simple Subject"): The core subject is the single noun or pronoun that forms the subject.

Complete Subject: The complete subject is the subject together with any adjectives or adjectival phrases modifying it.

e.g. The lady in the huge hat went to the market to buy groceries.

The core subject is *lady* and the complete subject is *the lady in the huge hat*.

OBJECT

An object is something or someone towards which an action or feeling is directed. In grammar an object is the thing, person, or quality affected by the action of the verb. (To put it another way, it receives the action of the verb.) Like a subject, an object normally is made up of a noun or pronoun.

Direct object: The direct object is the thing, person, or quality directly affected by the action of the verb. A direct object usually answers the question "What...?" or "Who...?". Notice that direct objects are <u>not</u> introduced by prepositions.

Indirect object: The indirect object is the thing, person, or quality that is <u>indirectly</u> affected by the action of the verb. All indirect objects *could be* expressed by making them the objects of the prepositions *to* or *for*. But the prepositions are often omitted. Indirect objects answer the questions "To whom?" and "For whom?".

Guerrero hit the ball a long way.

(Who did he hit? *The ball. The ball* is the direct object of the verb *hit*.)

She threw me her hat.

(What did she throw? *Her hat. Her hat* is the direct object. To whom did she throw it? *To me. Me* is the indirect object. Note that the sentence could be rephrased, "She threw her hat to me.")

They gave a watch to their father for Christmas.

(direct object is *watch*; indirect object is *father*)

PREDICATE

The predicate is everything that is said about the subject. In the example on page 223, "went to the market to buy groceries" is the predicate. A predicate always includes a verb.

CLAUSE

A distinct group of words that includes both a subject and a predicate. Thus a clause always includes a verb.

PHRASE

A distinct group of words that does not include both a subject and a verb. Examples:

CLAUSES	PHRASES
because he is strong	because of his strength (no verb)
before she comes home	before the meeting (no verb)
the professor likes me	from Halifax
a tree fell down	a beautiful face
who came to dinner	in the evening

TYPES OF CLAUSES

Main Clause

A main clause is a group of words which is, <u>or could be</u>, a sentence on its own.

Subordinate Clause

A subordinate clause is a clause which could <u>not</u> form a complete sentence on its own.

Except for the coordinating conjunctions (*and, but, for, nor, or, so,* and *yet*), conjunctions do not introduce main clauses, so if a clause begins with a word such as *because, although, after,* or *if,* you can be confident it is a subordinate clause. Similarly, relative pronouns introduce subordinate clauses—never main clauses.

> She lives near Pittsburgh.
>
> (One main clause forming a complete sentence. The pronoun *She* is the subject, *lives* is the verb, and the preposition *near* and the noun *Pittsburgh* together form a phrase.)

He danced in the street because he was feeling happy.

main clause: He danced in the street
subject:_____
verb:_____
subordinate clause: because he was feeling happy
subject:_____
verb:_____

Mavis has married a man who is older than her father.

main clause: Mavis has married a man
subject:_____
verb:_____
subordinate clause: who is older than her father
subject: _____
verb: _____

TYPES OF SUBORDINATE CLAUSES

Clause Types

Adjectival subordinate clause: a subordinate clause that tells us more about a noun or pronoun. Adjectival clauses begin with relative pronouns such as *who, whom, whose, which,* and *that.*

Adverbial subordinate clause: a subordinate clause that tells us more about the action of a verb—telling how, when, why, or where the action occurred.

Noun subordinate clause: a clause that acts like a noun to form the subject or object of a sentence.

Examples:

He talked at length to his cousin, who quickly became bored.
("Who quickly became bored" is an adjectival subordinate clause telling us more about the noun *cousin.*)

My husband did not like the gift that I gave him.
("That I gave him" is an adjectival subordinate clause telling us more about the noun *gift.*)

The boy whom she wants to marry is very poor.
("Whom she wants to marry" is an adjectival subordinate clause telling us more about the noun *boy.* Notice that here the subordinate clause appears <u>in the middle of</u> the main clause "The boy is very poor.")

I felt worse after I had been to the doctor.
("After I had been to the doctor" is an adverbial subordinate clause telling <u>when</u> I felt worse.)

He could not attend because he had broken his leg.
("Because he had broken his leg" is an adverbial subordinate clause telling <u>why</u> he could not attend.)

She jumped as if an alarm had sounded.

("as if an alarm had sounded" is an adverbial subordinate clause telling <u>how</u> she jumped.)

What he said was very interesting.

("What he said" is a noun clause acting as the subject of the sentence, in the same way that the noun *conversation* acts as the subject in "The conversation was very interesting.")

Sue-Ellen told me that she wanted to become a lawyer.

("That she wanted to become a lawyer" is a noun clause acting as the object, in the same way that the noun *plans* acts as the object in "Sue-Ellen told me her plans.")

TYPES OF PHRASES

Adjectival phrase: a phrase that tells us more about a noun or pronoun.

Adverbial phrase: a phrase that tells us more about the action of a verb, answering questions such as "When...?", "Where...?", "How...?", and "Why...?".

The boy in the new jacket got into the car.

("In the new jacket" is an adjectival phrase telling us more about the noun *boy*.)

I drank from the cup with a broken handle.

("With a broken handle" is an adjectival phrase telling us more about the noun *cup*.)

We went to the park.

("To the park" is an adverbial phrase telling <u>where</u> we went.)

They arrived after breakfast.

("After breakfast" is an adverbial phrase telling <u>when</u> they arrived.)

PHRASES AND CLAUSES

They were late because of the weather.

("Because of the weather" is an adverbial phrase telling us <u>why</u> they were late. It has no verb.)

They were late because the weather was bad.

("Because the weather was bad" is an adverbial clause telling us why they were late.)

The man at the corner appeared to be drunk.

("At the corner" is an adjectival phrase telling us more about the noun *man*.)

The man who stood at the corner appeared to be drunk.

("Who stood at the corner" is an adjectival clause telling us more about the noun *man*.)

Parts of Speech and Parts of the Sentence

Example:
After the generous man with the big ears has bought presents, he will quickly give them to his friends.

PARTS OF SPEECH:

after: conjunction

generous:_____

with: _____

big: _____

has bought:_____

he:_____

quickly:_____

to:_____

friends:_____

the: article

man:_____

the:_____

ears: _____

presents:_____

will give:_____

them:_____

his:_____

Parts of the Sentence

main clause: He will quickly give them to his friends.
subject:_____
predicate:_____
verb:_____
direct object:_____
indirect object:_____

subordinate clause: After the generous man with the big ears has bought presents
Is this an adjectival or an adverbial subordinate clause?
core subject: the noun _____
complete
subject:_____
adjectival phrase: with the big ears
This phrase tells us more about the noun: _____
predicate:_____
direct object:_____

APPENDIX 2:
CORRECTION KEY

Ab	Faulty abbreviation
Adj	Improper use of adjective
Adv	Improper use of adverb
Agr	Faulty agreement
Amb	Ambiguous
Awk	Awkward expression or construction
Cap	Faulty capitalization
CS	Comma splice
D	Faulty diction
Dgl	Dangling construction
Frag	Fragment
lc	Use lowercase
Num	Error in use of numbers
||	Lack of parallelism
P	Faulty punctuation
Ref	Unclear pronoun reference
Rep	Unnecessary repetition
R-O	Run-on
Sp	Error in spelling
SS	Faulty sentence structure
T	Wrong tense of verb
tr ∿	Transpose elements (e.g., to quickly go, recieye)
V	Wrong verb form
Wdy	Wordy
˅	Add apostrophe or single quotation mark
⌒	Close up
⌄	Add comma
ℓ	Delete
∧	Insert
¶	Begin a new paragraph
No ¶	Do not begin a new paragraph
⊙	Add a period
˅ ˅	Double quotation marks
#	Add space

INDEX

LIST
of products used:

457 lb(s) of Rolland Enviro100 Print
100% post-consumer

RESULTS
Based on the Cascades products you selected
compared to products in the industry made with
100% virgin fiber, your savings are:

4 trees

3,781 gal. US of water
41 days of water consumption

478 lbs of waste
4 waste containers

1,242 lbs CO2
2.356 miles driven

6 MMBTU
29,464 60W light bulbs for one hour

4 lbs NOx
emissions of one truck during 5
days

RECYCLED
Paper made from
recycled material
FSC
www.fsc.org
FSC® C103567